SMOKERAMA

rettes by mail and have them shipped to you by Pa[r]
Post.

Cigarettes are sold only by the carton. Each car[ton]
contains a total of 200 cigarettes. We do not sell [less]
than a carton. Please note that we receive fresh st[ock]
of cigarettes almost daily, thus avoioding the dan[ger]
of giving you stale "shelf" cigarettes. **Prices sh[own]
below do not include postage which is extra** and m[ust]
be added to your remittance. Otherwise cigarettes [are]
sent by Express collect. Average shipping weight [of]
each carton is one pound.

No. 9148. WINGS (New L[arge] Size), Per Carton..$
No. 9149. MARVEL, Per [Carton]
No. 9154. CAMEL, Per [Carton]
No. 9155. LUCKY STRIKE, [Per] Carton.
No. 9156. CHESTERFIELD, [Pe]r Carton.
No. 9157. OLD GOLD, P[er] Car[ton]
No. 9144. [R]ALEIGH, [Per] Carton
No. 9162. [KOOL] MENTHOL, Per Carton.
No. 9166. [PA]LL [MA]LL, Per Carton.
No. 917[0.] [SPU]R, Per Carton.
No. 914[3.] [H]ERBERT TAREYTON, P[er Ca]rton
No. 914[7. VI]CEROY, Per Carton.
No. 9176. MARLBORO, Per Carton..

MURAD TURKISH BLEND C[IGAR]ETTES

Those who appreciat[e] the excellent Turkish b[lend pref]er them to
other kinds. For a n[ew] smoking thrill, try a c[arton of] Murads. [200]
cigarettes per carton, p[a]ckaged 20 cigarettes p[er king] size box.
No. 9168. MURAD [TUR]K[ISH BLEND]
Per Carton............ $3.[ ]

ENG[LISH] OVALS CIGA[RETT]ES

For smooth, mild[sm]o[kin]g try this famous [b]lend. Ovals [are]
famous the world ov[er. Car]ton of 200 cigarette[s,] 20 to cr[ush]
proof-box.
No. 9145. ENGLIS[H O]VALS. Per Carton..... $2.[ ]

SANO (NICOTINE REMOVED) CIGARETTES

For healthier smoking, we recommend Sano cigarettes. Same en[joy]
able smoking from fine quality tobaccos with most of the nicotine [re]
moved $2.[ ]

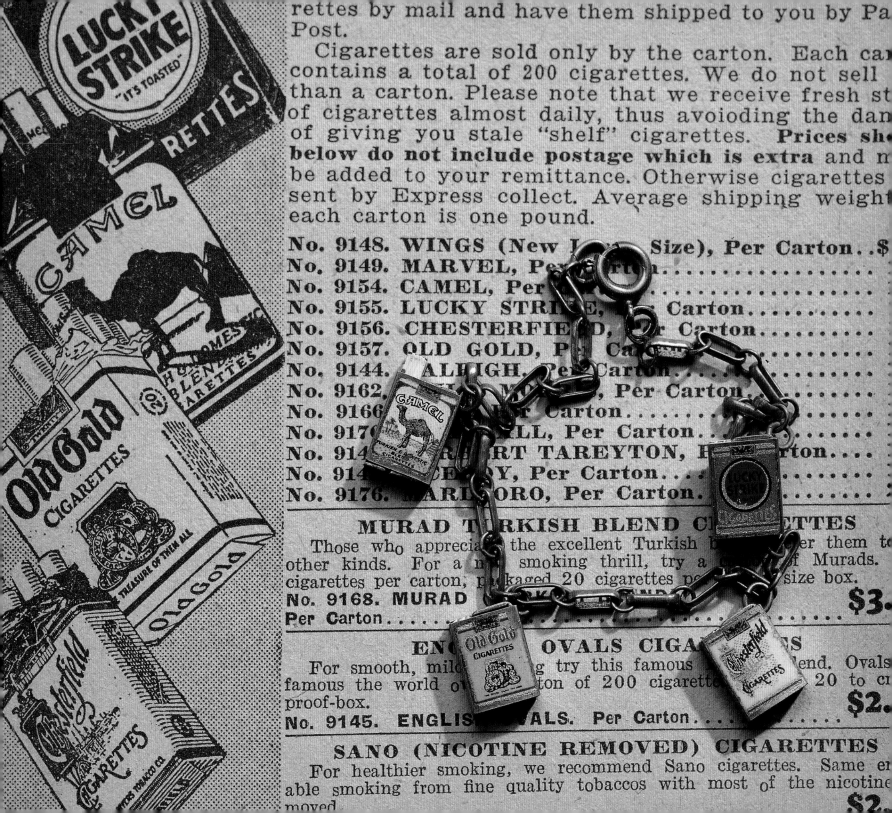

PHILIP COLLINS

SMOKERAMA

CLASSIC TOBACCO ACCOUTREMENTS

PHOTOGRAPHY BY

SAM SARGENT

CHRONICLE BOOKS • SAN FRANCISCO

A Fillip Book

Text copyright © 1992 by Fillip Films Inc.

Photo composition by Philip Collins.

Printed in Hong Kong.

Library of Congress Cataloging in Publication Data.

Collins, Philip, 1944-

Smokerama : classic tobacco accoutrements / Philip Collins ; photography by Sam Sargent.
p. cm.

"A Fillip book."

ISBN 0-8118-0119-5 (pbk.)

1. Smoking paraphernalia—History. I. Sargent, Sam. II. Title.
TS2280.C65 1992
688' .4—dc20   92-1007   CIP

Editing: Chuck Robbins
Book and cover design:
Visual Strategies [ViS], San Francisco
Cover photograph: Sam Sargent

Distributed in Canada by
Raincoast Books
112 East Third Avenue
Vancouver, B.C. V5T 1C8

10 9 8 7 6 5 4 3 2 1

Chronicle Books
275 Fifth Street
San Francisco, California 94103

PHOTO OPPOSITE TITLE PAGE: A CHARM BRACELET FROM THE MID-THIRTIES FEATURES DELICATE REPRODUCTIONS OF FOUR POPULAR CIGARETTE PACK DESIGNS, AUTHENTIC IN GRAPHICS DETAIL AND COLOR. THEY MEASURE 3/8" BY 1/4". ENAMEL ON BRASS. MINUTIA OF EXPOSED CIGARETTES AT THE TOP OF THE PACKS CONTRIBUTE SIGNIFICANTLY TO THEIR APPEAL. *KAY TORNBORG COLLECTION.*

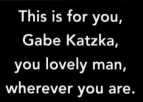

This is for you,
Gabe Katzka,
you lovely man,
wherever you are.

Generous thanks are due to all the contributors whose names appear in this book. Particular thanks to Kay Tornborg, Sam Sargent, Baron Wolman, Mary Merrick, and Dick Stettler.

Special mentions are due to those who cheerfully complied with requests beyond "reasonable:" Noel Barrett, June Berliner, "Tobacco Bill" Hatcher, Peter Linden, John McKenna, Eric Menard, Frank Piccolo, Barry Reynolds, and Harvey Schwartz.

Once upon a time, smoking—particularly cigarette smoking—was considered a chic and sophisticated mannerism. Following World War I, cigarettes were introduced to millions of consumers through contemporary advertising and modern marketing methods. Throughout the twenties, thirties, and forties, in films, novels, and popular stories, cigarettes were associated with images of pleasure and fulfillment. ¶ Cigarette companies fostered glamour, mystery, and romance in their package design and advertising, producing an amazing variety of seductive reasons to smoke. In countless magazine advertisements, radio commercials, and cigarette pack designs, the mystique of smoking was evoked. ¶ The wide-spread use of tobacco products in this century spawned an enormous demand for accessories to facilitate smoking. Companies achieved international status in providing a spectacular array of products to please the eye while yet performing a function beyond the merely decorative. Over the years, smoking accessories, which had been created initially as mere accoutrements to the process of smoking, became objects of consumption in their own right. ¶ The following pages illustrate only a fraction of the beautiful, interesting, and quirky objects that became standard personal and household artifacts for the smoker. Lighters from Zippo and Ronson became as familiar as table cutlery in American homes. Tiffany, Cartier, Chase, and Dunhill catered to the smoker, producing a range of classically styled lighters, cases, and boxes that have become today's collectibles. ¶ Lighters and cigarette cases became a standard for personalized gifts, invariably providing a flat surface that could be monogrammed. Generally mass produced, these items became famous for their quality and durability. The Zippo manufacturing company still offers a lifetime guarantee on its lighter, a product that has become a legend in the United States. ¶ Novelty items for dispensing cigarettes also proliferated. Lighters were housed in an extraordinary variety of cases, from the obvious detonator box to whimsical contraptions that sent sparks flying across the horns of a devil. Ashtrays came in an equally astonishing range. Most reception areas, waiting rooms, lounges, elevator entrances, and lobbies provided ashstands or ashtrays, usually purveying a tobacco product in word or form. ¶ Hotels and restaurants, radio stations and service stations advertised themselves on personalized ashtrays that were generally produced at very low cost in anticipation of light-fingered souvenir hunters. Then, as now, matchbooks carrying advertising slogans were given away at no charge. ¶ As women acquired the right to vote, they also acquired the attention of designers and advertisers who saw a great, untapped market. Presentation sets of lighter, cigarette case, and compact, as well as other smoking accessories, became household decorations and objects for making personal design statements. ¶ It is doubtful that any other industry has spawned as many allied consumer products. Dashes of elegance and bursts of frivolity are interwoven in the design of the products on the following pages. In today's butane-fired world, the flint and wheel, petrol-fueled lighter is an anachronism that is currently enjoying a rebirth—as a decorative collectible. ¶ These objects echo a vast industry—and way of life—forever changed by scientific inquiry into the effects of smoking upon our health. Nonetheless, in the early decades of the twentieth century, smoking was a seemingly natural adjunct to glamorous living, and the possession of these accessories another example of sophistication and good taste.

3

An all-metal profile of a dapper and correct smoker modeled as a **cigarette dispenser**, c. 1928. Depress the spotted bow tie, and a cigarette appears at the lips. Cigarettes are stored horizontally, inside the face. German. *Kay Tornborg Collection.*

4

CIGARETTES ARE STORED IN A CIRCULAR **storage cannister** BEHIND THE FACE OF THE FLAPPER.

THE HEADBAND IS OF FELT AND SILK. WHEN THE BUTTON IS PUSHED TO THE LEFT, A SINGLE CIGARETTE APPEARS AT HER LIPS.

WOOD CABINET AND MOLDED PRESSED WOOD FACE, U.S., C. 1920. *THOMAS A. GRAY COLLECTION.*

AN EARLY THIRTIES **English cigarette box** IN BLACK PHENOLIC, MOTTLED WITH RED AND GREEN (LEFT), AND AN ENGLISH BOX MANUFACTURED IN UREA FORMALDEHYDE, A CREAM PLASTIC, WITH BLUE-GREEN GRAINED LEATHERETTE PANELS (RIGHT). THE ROLL TOP THRUSTS FIVE SPLAYED FINGERS OFFERING CIGARETTES FROM AN INTERIOR STORE OF APPROXIMATELY TWENTY. MANUFACTURED IN THE EARLY FIFTIES BY ROLINX. *AUTHOR COLLECTION.*

A SUNBURST OF CIGARETTES IS OFFERED WHEN THE NECKS OF THESE BOTTLES ARE EXTENDED. **Japanese novelties**, C.1960. THE **Hennessy bottle** SPORTS A SIMPLE LIGHTER IN THE TOP AND IS MANUFACTURED IN COMPRESSION MOLDED PLASTIC AKIN TO **Bakelite** (LEFT). THE **Moët Champagne bottle** IS ALL METAL. *DICK STETTLER COLLECTION.*

8

SIX COLORFUL **ladies' cigarette holders** FROM THE THIRTIES FAN OVER AN ORNATE STERLING SILVER BRAIDED PATTERNED HOLDER OF UNKNOWN ORIGIN WITH ITS ORIGINAL FELT-LINED LEATHER CASE, C. 1920. THE EXOTIC SCOTTIE DOG CIGARETTE HOLDER WAS PROBABLY PRODUCED DURING "FALAMANIA" TIME, WHEN THE WHITE HOUSE DOG, FALA, EQUALLED HIS MASTER, FRANKLIN DELANO ROOSEVELT, IN POPULARITY. PRODUCED IN TRANSLUCENT PHENOLIC PLASTIC. *JUNE BERLINER COLLECTION.*

A curious **cigarette holder** design theme was to have reflected class and status among women of the twenties and thirties. The longer and slimmer the holder, the more confident (and up-market) the smoker appeared. Usually the prerogative of the leisured class, some holders expanded to extraordinary lengths, as long as fourteen inches, or contracted to "normal" size. Tortoise shell and other colored plastics were a popular choice. U.S., c. 1930.

June Berliner Collection.

9

A STERLING SILVER SET, FROM AUSTRIA,

ENAMELLED WITH A PORTRAIT OF PHARAOH

MIENPTAH-HOTEPHIMAT, NECROPOLIS OF

THEBES, NINETEENTH DYNASTY. THE

lighter/compact/cigarette case

SET WAS FORMERLY OWNED BY PRINCESS

FAWZIA, FIRST WIFE OF THE SHAH OF IRAN AND

SISTER OF EGYPT'S KING FAROUK. THE TWO-

PIECE SET IN CLASSIC ART DECO MOTIF BEARS

THE GOLDEN WHEEL LOGO, PATENTED IN 1929.

JUNE BERLINER COLLECTION.

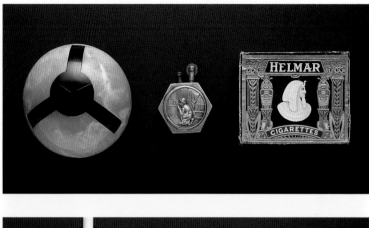

THE **art deco "Tennis ball" ashtray** WAS MANUFACTURED IN
ENGLAND, C. 1935, BY ROANOID LTD., A MOLDING COMPANY FOR DUNLOP
RUBBER (LEFT). THE BODY IS UREA FORMALDEHYDE, AND THE ARMS, PHENOL
FORMALDEHYDE. SEVERAL COLOR VARIATIONS WERE PRODUCED. A HANDMADE
"TRENCH ART" WHEEL AND FLINT LIGHTER, MADE IN 1917, FEATURES A KEYHOLE
PEEPER AND HIS SUBJECT. ENGLISH (CENTER). ¶ HELMAR CIGARETTES BORE POPULAR
EGYPTIAN PHARAOH GRAPHICS AS THEIR PACK ART IN THE MID-TWENTIES (RIGHT).
HELMAR WAS A BRAND NAME FROM LORILLARD TOBACCO CO.
CENTER AND LEFT, JUNE BERLINER COLLECTION. RIGHT, KAY TORNBORG COLLECTION.

A SLIGHTLY STYLIZED VISION OF
THE FAMILIAR LOGO ADORNS THE
**ceramic cigarette
holder**, MANUFACTURED BY
HENRIOT QUIMPER, FRANCE,
IN THE MID-THIRTIES.
THOMAS A. GRAY COLLECTION.

12

An **automaton**, MANUFACTURED IN FRANCE IN THE LATE 1940S, ECHOES THE DESIGN OF ITS NINETEENTH-CENTURY PREDECESSOR. THIS VERSION IS ELECTRICALLY POWERED, OPERATING A CONCEALED BELLOWS THAT "SMOKES" THE VERTICAL CIGARETTE IN THE HOOKAH, CAUSING THE BABY-FACED, BEARDED SMOKER TO PUFF SMOKE FROM HIS MOUTH. AT THE SAME TIME, THE LEFT HAND OSCILLATES TO AND FRO, CAUSING A SLIGHT AIR CURRENT FROM THE FAN TO CLEAR THE SMOKE. THE RIGHT HAND LIFTS THE PIPE TO HIS MOUTH, AS HIS HEAD IS TURNING FROM RIGHT TO LEFT. *COURTESY: OFF THE WALL, MELROSE AVENUE.*

13

14

A **brass cigarette pack holder** FEATURING THE FAMOUS CAMEL, THE MOST WIDELY RECOGNIZED CIGARETTE LOGO IN THE WORLD. MANUFACTURED IN 1920, THIS BRASS EXAMPLE IS ONE OF THE MANY STYLES THAT PROMOTED THE CAMEL. EIGHTY-SEVEN YEARS LATER THE CAMEL CIGARETTE IS STILL AVAILABLE IN THE FAMILIAR R.J. REYNOLDS PACK.

COURTESY, R.J. REYNOLDS COLLECTION.

15

TWO BRASS CAMELS SUPPORT A **cigarette holder** FOR TEN CIGARETTES. PROBABLY OF EGYPTIAN MANUFACTURE, C. 1925. IT IS UNKNOWN WHETHER THE DESIGN WAS INSPIRED BY THE R.J. REYNOLDS CIGARETTE LOGO, OR THE LOCAL FORM OF TRANSPORT. THOMAS A. GRAY COLLECTION.

THE AUTO COLLECTION **cigarette cards** WERE OFFERED BY TURKEY RED CIGARETTES. THEY SERVED AS PACK STIFFENERS AS WELL AS AN INDUCEMENT TO COLLECT THE COMPLETE SET, C. 1915–1920. *CLETUS WRIGHT COLLECTION.*

16

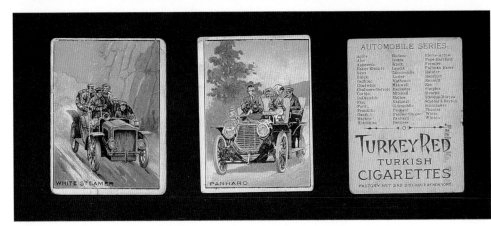

THE HISTORY OF AMERICAN ADVERTISING IS PUNCTUATED WITH FAMOUS CAMPAIGNS THAT PRODUCED SUCCESS FOR THEIR PRODUCTS AND CLIENTS. A HIGH PROPORTION OF THESE WERE SPONSORED BY CIGARETTE COMPANIES AND THEIR ADVERTISING AGENCIES WHO, FROM THE TURN OF THE CENTURY UNTIL THE PRESENT, HAVE PRODUCED CAMPAIGNS HAVING SIGNIFICANT POTENCY AND BRILLIANT IMAGERY.

18

19

A **novelty cigarette dispenser** FROM THE TWENTIES, FROM SCHWARTZBAUGH MANUFACTURING COMPANY, TOLEDO, OHIO. DEPRESS THE MULE'S EAR AND PRESTO!—A CIGARETTE APPEARS. PAINTED METAL. *DICK STETTLER COLLECTION.*

Personalized cigarette cases (GENERALLY WITH NAMES OR INITIALS) HAVE MADE GREAT GIFT-GIVING IDEAS FOR OVER A HUNDRED YEARS. THIS EXAMPLE TRANSCENDS THE NORMAL FORM. THE CASE, IN STERLING SILVER WITH ROSE GOLD ON THE FACE SIDE, WAS GIVEN TO A RUSSIAN ARMY OFFICER, "THE WOLF," BY TWO LADIES, MARSYA AND MARUSSA. AMONG VARIOUS TEXTS APPEARS THE LEGEND, "IF YOU LIVE LIKE A WOLF, YOU BARK LIKE A WOLF." THE WOLF'S HEAD HAS RUBY EYES AND A NUGGET OF GOLD ABOVE. ¶ THE RECIPIENT, PROBABLY A RUSSIAN NOBLEMAN, WAS CHARACTERIZED BY VARIOUS CUSTOMIZED SYMBOLS APPEARING ON THE BACK OF THE CASE. THE RUSSIAN IMPERIAL FLAG IS REPRESENTED, AND "54" WAS PROBABLY A REGIMENT IDENTITY NUMBER. PLAYING CARDS, DEER, AND RABBITS SUGGEST SPORTING ACTIVITIES, WHILE OTHER SYMBOLS OFFER IMAGINATIVE POSSIBILITIES. IT WAS PROBABLE THAT, BEING THE RECIPIENT OF A SINGLE GIFT FROM TWO LADIES, THE WOLF LED A FULL AND EXCITING LIFE IN 1908.

JUNE BERLINER COLLECTION.

21

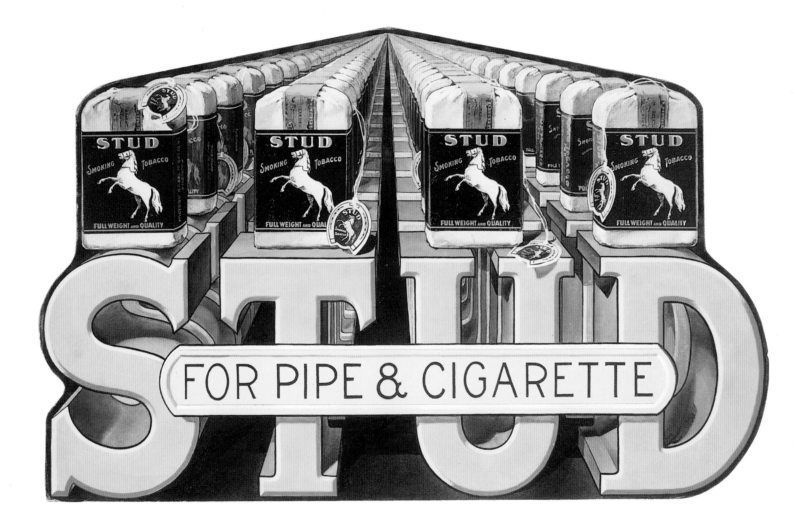

"Stud" counter and window display graphics UNDERLINE THE ATTENTION-GRABBING PROPERTIES OF SUPERIOR ARTWORK, C. 1910.

Czechoslovakian unglazed ceramic ashtray FROM 1936. AN INTERESTING AND CURIOUS COMBINATION OF TYROLIAN HAT AND MARCEL WAVED HAIR. KAY TORNBORG COLLECTION.

24

A **table lighter, flint and wheel mechanism**, MOLDED IN LUCITE, MANUFACTURED BY STRIKE-A-LITE, NEW YORK, C. 1938. URBAN CUMMINGS COLLECTION.

A **Baccarat crystal ashtray** FEATURING AN ELEGANT, FANCIFUL ETCHED SMOKING

IMAGE REFLECTED FROM THE BASE. FRENCH, C. 1930. *JUNE BERLINER COLLECTION.*

Male-oriented smoking accessories. A Japanese "Temptation" cigarette case engraved with a scantily clad sheik and harem girl from the forties (top left). A "Miss Cutie" plastic lighter by Negbaur, New York, from the fifties (top right). A propelling pencil and lighter from Automet (USA), made in the forties (bottom left). A combination lighter and ashtray that is concealed in the base and slides out to provide a spring-loaded cigarette 'rest'. Chromium-plated brass, flint, and wheel mechanism from Simpson, West Germany, c. 1950 (bottom right). *Top left and right, and bottom left, courtesy: Off The Wall, Los Angeles.* • *Bottom right: June Berliner Collection.*

26

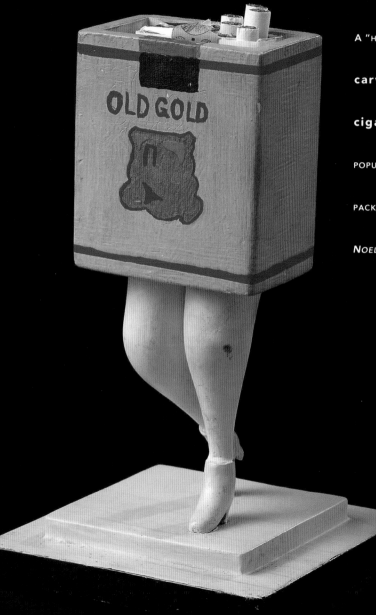

A "HOMEBREW," hand-
carved wooden
cigarette box OF THE
POPULAR OLD GOLD DANCING
PACKS. U.S., LATE FORTIES.

NOEL BARRETT COLLECTION.

Lighters FOR TABLES OF THE THIRTIES FEATURED STATUESQUE DANCERS STRAINING IN IMPROBABLE POSES (LEFT AND RIGHT). A) "SILENT FLAME" TOUCH-TIP "ELECTRIC" LIGHTER IN CHROME AND BAKELITE WITH BRASS RAILS BY PARKER OF LONDON, ENGLAND. B) GERMAN TUBE LIGHTER FEATURING BRASS BATHING BELLE, C. 1912. C) BRASS TUBE LIGHTER (FLINT AND WHEEL MECHANISM MANUFACTURED BY R. & F. COMPANY), C. 1930. D) DUNHILL (USA) "SILENT FLAME" TOUCH-TIP "ELECTRIC" LIGHTER. METAL ON BAKELITE BASE WITH BRASS RAILS. THE TOUCH-TIP FLAME IGNITION IS ACHIEVED BY TOUCHING THE TIP OF THE EXTRACTED IGNITER ROD ON WHATEVER PART OF THE METAL LADY'S ANATOMY IS DEEMED APPROPRIATE. *JUNE BERLINER COLLECTION.*

28

A

B

C

D

A **standing bronzed metal ashtray** IN THE STYLE OF ARTHUR VON FRANKENBURG'S NUDIE NYMPHET STATUARY (FRANKART). MANUFACTURED IN THE EARLY TWENTIES, THIS EXAMPLE WAS MADE BY ART METAL CREATIONS, NEW YORK. *KAY TORNBORG COLLECTION.*

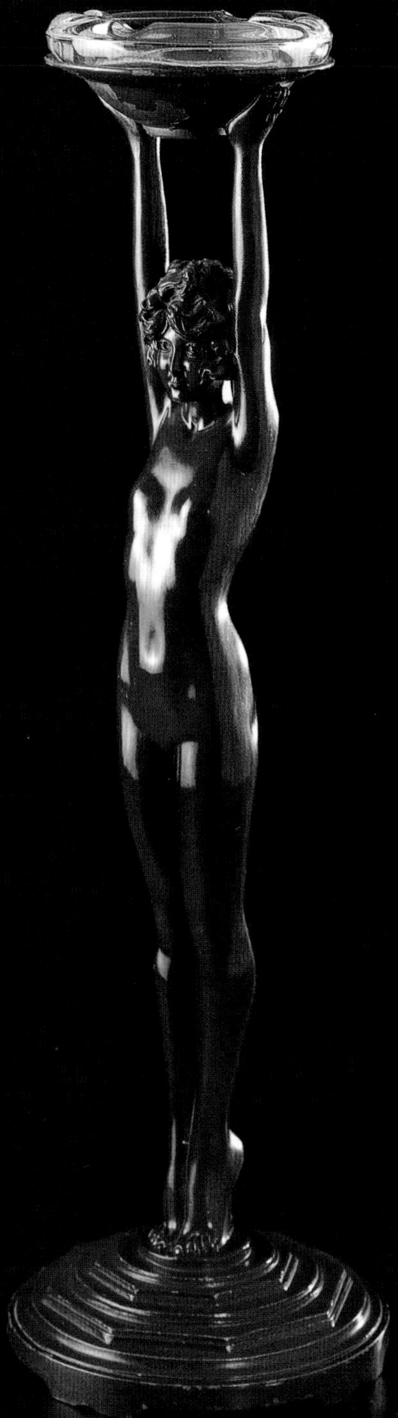

RED RHINESTONES ADORN A NUBILE BASKET BEARER CARRYING AN **Evans lighter** WITH FLINT AND WHEEL MECHANISM, C. 1938 (LEFT). THE **Dunhill "Hunting Horn" lighter** FOR TABLE USE IN COPPER AND BRASS IS CONSIDERED A CLASSIC BY COLLECTORS (RIGHT). ENGLAND, C. 1936. *JUNE BERLINER COLLECTION.*

32

At the turn of the century, cigarette companies were anxious to reach women smokers. Women were wooed with the inclusion of illustrated "silks," or satin inserts, in cigarette packs. The silks were generally confined to the size parameter of the pack but larger size silks were available directly from the tobacco companies with evidence of a purchase of their products by the applicant.

Cletus Wright Collection.

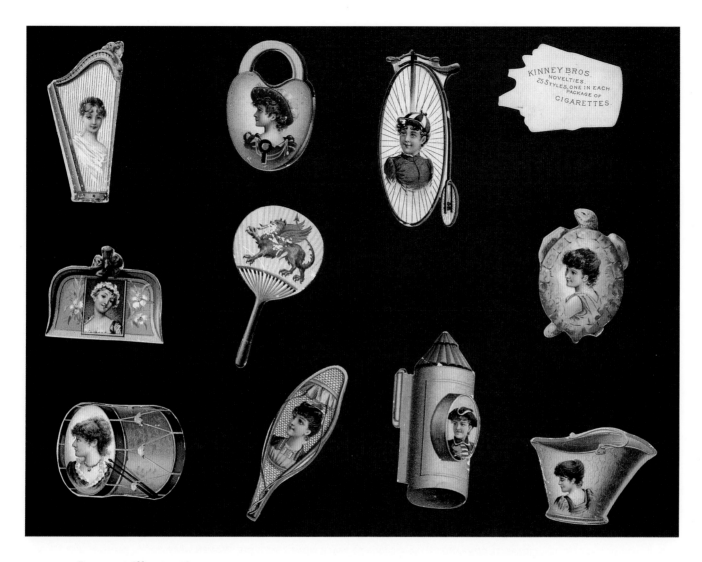

On the image, in the top right card: KINNEY BROS. NOVELTIES. 25 STYLES, ONE IN EACH PACKAGE OF CIGARETTES

Dye cut illustrations, AS ALTERNATIVES TO SILKS, WERE OFFERED IN AN EFFORT TO ATTRACT THE FEMALE SMOKER

TO A BRAND. THEY FEATURED SETS OF 25, 30, AND 50 IMAGES. FULL COLOR PRINTING ON A STOUT CARD ENSURED A LONG LIFE FOR

THE EXQUISITE ILLUSTRATIONS, C. 1900–1915.

CLETUS WRIGHT COLLECTION.

IMAGES OF COWBOYS AND INDIANS WERE TRADITIONAL FOR **cigarette card** COLLECTORS. THESE ILLUSTRATIONS WERE INCLUDED IN PACKS OF HASSAN CORKTIP CIGARETTES, "THE ORIENTAL SMOKE," BILLED AS "THE LARGEST SELLING BRAND OF CIGARETTES IN AMERICA." C. 1910–1915. *CLETUS WRIGHT COLLECTION.*

35

JIGGS AND MISS AMERICA FACE BOOB MCNUTT, A RUBE GOLDBERG
CHARACTER. STANDING 3 FEET HIGH, THESE **wood ashstands**,
OF U.S. MANUFACTURE, FEATURED FAMOUS FICTIONAL (AND SOME-
TIMES REAL) CHARACTERS. THEY FORESHADOWED THE EXTENSIVE PER-
SONAL ENDORSEMENT ADVERTISING UNDERTAKEN BY MAJOR TOBAC-
CO COMPANIES THROUGHOUT THE FORTIES AND FIFTIES.
NOEL BARRETT COLLECTION.

A **German children's**
dexterity puzzle, THIS FEATURES A MIRROR
ON THE REVERSE SIDE AND IS DESIGNED TO INFURIATE
THE MOST PATIENT PLAYER. A TINY CIGARETTE ROLLS
FREELY AROUND THE SURFACE OF THE IMAGE. THE
OBJECT OF THE PUZZLE IS TO COAX THE CIGARETTE
INTO THE CARPENTER'S LIPS, C. 1935.
AUTHOR COLLECTION.

JIGGS (LEFT) AND POPEYE ARE EXAMPLES OF **novelty ashstands** THAT
BECAME POPULAR IN THE THIRTIES. AT APPROXIMATELY 3 FEET HIGH, THEY ARE
CONVENIENTLY AT CHAIRSIDE HEIGHT. MADE OF CARVED, PAINTED WOOD. U.S.
NOEL BARRETT COLLECTION.

38

DOES
**"THUNDER
ON THE TRACK"
SPEED YOUR
CIGARETTES?**

*Then you'll want
that
Cleaner Taste!*

When thoroughbreds thunder into the home stretch and things you hope for are in the balance by a nose... do your cigarettes take up the pace? That's the time to learn that Spud is a thoroughbred too! For Spud's cooler smoke always leaves your mouth moist-cool and comfortably clean, no matter how long or concentrated your session with its lusty tobacco fragrance. Occasional smoker or 2-pack-a-day smoker, Spud is the "mouth-happy" cigarette... the grand new freedom in old-fashioned tobacco enjoyment.

SPUD
MENTHOL-COOLED
CIGARETTES
20 FOR 20c (U.S.)...20 FOR 30c (CANADA)

THE AXTON-FISHER TOBACCO COMPANY, INC., LOUISVILLE, KENTUCKY

39

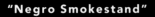

"Negro Smokestand"

MANUFACTURED BY "THE SCHLESINGER

LINE OF DISTINCTION" IN 1923. PAINTED

METAL WITH BRASS CIGARETTE CONTAINER,

ASHTRAY, AND MATCH HOLDER.

COURTESY: HARVEY'S, MELROSE AVENUE.

THE COON CHICKEN INN, WITH 3 LOCATIONS IN SEATTLE, PORTLAND, AND SALT LAKE CITY, EPITOMIZED AMERICAN ENTREPRENEURIAL TALENT. FOUNDED IN SEATTLE IN 1923, THE RESTAURANTS SERVED FAMILY FARE UNTIL THEIR CLOSURE IN 1943. THE OWNER, M.L. GRAHAM, MERCHANDISED HIS RESTAURANT LOGO IN GRAND STYLE, INCORPORATING GIFT SHOPS THAT SOLD AN ENORMOUS RANGE OF COON CHICKEN MEMORABILIA AND GIFT ITEMS IMPRINTED WITH THE RESTAURANT LOGO. THE **book matches, match holders** AND **strikers**, AND **cigarette jar** WERE ALL PURCHASED FROM THE GIFT SHOP. ITEMS AS DIVERSE AS DINNER NAPKINS AND SPARE AUTO WHEEL COVERS WERE MODESTLY PRICED, AND ALL CARRIED THE FAMILIAR LOGO. *PETER LINDEN & ERIC MENARD COLLECTION.*

41

THE **Ronson Touch-Tip bar lighter** HAS BECOME A PRIZED COLLECTIBLE FOR TODAY'S ART DECO ADMIRERS (LEFT). REGULARLY AUCTIONED IN FINE ART

SPECIALIST SALES AND FIRST PRODUCED IN THE U.S. IN 1936, THIS JAZZY DESIGN EPITOMIZES "THE THIRTIES." THE **Junior Bartender**," A SIMILAR DESIGN,

PRESIDES OVER A CYLINDRICAL CANNISTER THAT CONTAINS CIGARETTES (CENTER). WHEN THE BAR IS LIFTED, A SPRAY OF CIGARETTES IS OFFERED.

MADE IN THE U.S., C. 1938. A **French cigarette dispenser** OF THE SAME PERIOD FEATURES A MIRROR IMAGE OF THE RONSON BARTENDER (RIGHT).

LEFT AND CENTER, JUNE BERLINER COLLECTION. RIGHT, COURTESY: PICCOLO PETE'S, SHERMAN OAKS.

42

Height 6 7/8"
Width 6"
Depth 2 3/4"

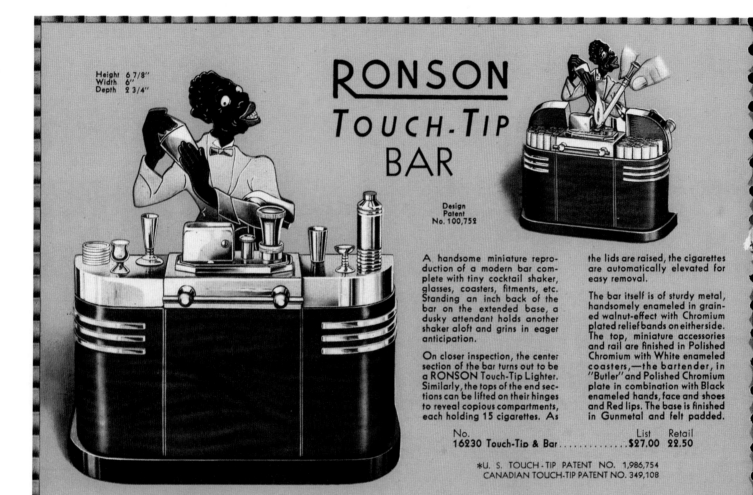

RONSON

TOUCH-TIP

BAR

Design
Patent
No. 100,752

A handsome miniature reproduction of a modern bar complete with tiny cocktail shaker, glasses, coasters, fitments, etc. Standing an inch back of the bar on the extended base, a dusky attendant holds another shaker aloft and grins in eager anticipation.

On closer inspection, the center section of the bar turns out to be a RONSON Touch-Tip Lighter. Similarly, the tops of the end sections can be lifted on their hinges to reveal copious compartments, each holding 15 cigarettes. As

the lids are raised, the cigarettes are automatically elevated for easy removal.

The bar itself is of sturdy metal, handsomely enameled in grained walnut-effect with Chromium plated relief bands on either side. The top, miniature accessories and rail are finished in Polished Chromium with White enameled coasters,—the bartender, in "Butler" and Polished Chromium plate in combination with Black enameled hands, face and shoes and Red lips. The base is finished in Gunmetal and felt padded.

No.		List	Retail
16230 Touch-Tip & Bar		$27.00	22.50

*U. S. TOUCH-TIP PATENT NO. 1,986,754
CANADIAN TOUCH-TIP PATENT NO. 349,108

Printed in U. S. A.—1070

44

A FINE PAPIER-MACHÉ FIGURE
GRIMACING UNDER THE LOAD OF
FOUR TIERS OF CIGARETTES OFFERED
FROM A BOX IN THE FORM OF STACKED
BOOKS. THIS UNWILLING **cigarette
server**, MEASURING OVER 2 FEET
HIGH, STOOD AT RESTAURANT EXIT
COUNTERS AND HAT CHECK STATIONS
FOR THE CONVENIENCE OF PATRONS.
OF GERMAN MANUFACTURE, IN THE
LATE TWENTIES, THE FIGURE PRE-DATES
PHILIP MORRIS' FAMOUS BELLHOP WHO
STARTED CALLING FOR PHILIP MORRIS
IN 1933.
NOEL BARRETT COLLECTION.

MAJOR TOBACCO COMPANIES INCREASED
THEIR RADIO-ADVERTISING TIME DURING
THE DEPRESSION YEARS. IN 1933, PHILIP
MORRIS INTRODUCED THEIR "CALL FOR
PHILIP MORRIS" SLOGAN DELIVERED BY
JOHNNY ROVENTINI PLAYING A BELLHOP.
THIS COLOR LITHO ILLUSTRATION OF
JOHNNY WAS A **point-of-sale**
advertisement FOR TOBACCONISTS'
COUNTER DISPLAYS. THE POPULAR LOGO
SPAWNED MANY IMITATION BELLHOP CHAR-
ACTERS WHO CARRIED A VARIETY OF SMOK-
ING AND OTHER PARAPHERNALIA.
AUTHOR COLLECTION.

45

BANDY, THE EXTENSIVELY ADVERTISED GENERAL ELECTRIC CHARACTER, GENERALLY SOLD RADIOS BUT HERE OFFERS A HELPING HAND FOR CIGARETTE ASHES. THIS **bandy ashtray** WAS CREATED IN 1929 OF PAINTED WOOD ON A WOOD BASE. BANDY ALSO APPEARED AS A TWENTY-INCH DOLL WITH ARTICULATED JOINTS, PRODUCED BY JOSEPH KALLUS FOR CAMEO DOLL PRODUCTS.

NOEL BARRETT COLLECTION.

STYLIZED BELLHOPS WERE A THIRTIES FAVORITE. THEY CARRIED
EVERYTHING FROM SALT AND PEPPER TO NOTEPADS, AND
NATURALLY, CIGARETTES AND MATCHES. BRASS AND PAINTED
METAL, THESE **bellhop cigarette carriers** MEASURE
6 INCHES AND 10-1/2 INCHES, RESPECTIVELY. *LEFT AND RIGHT,*
AUTHOR COLLECTION CENTER, JUNE BERLINER COLLECTION.

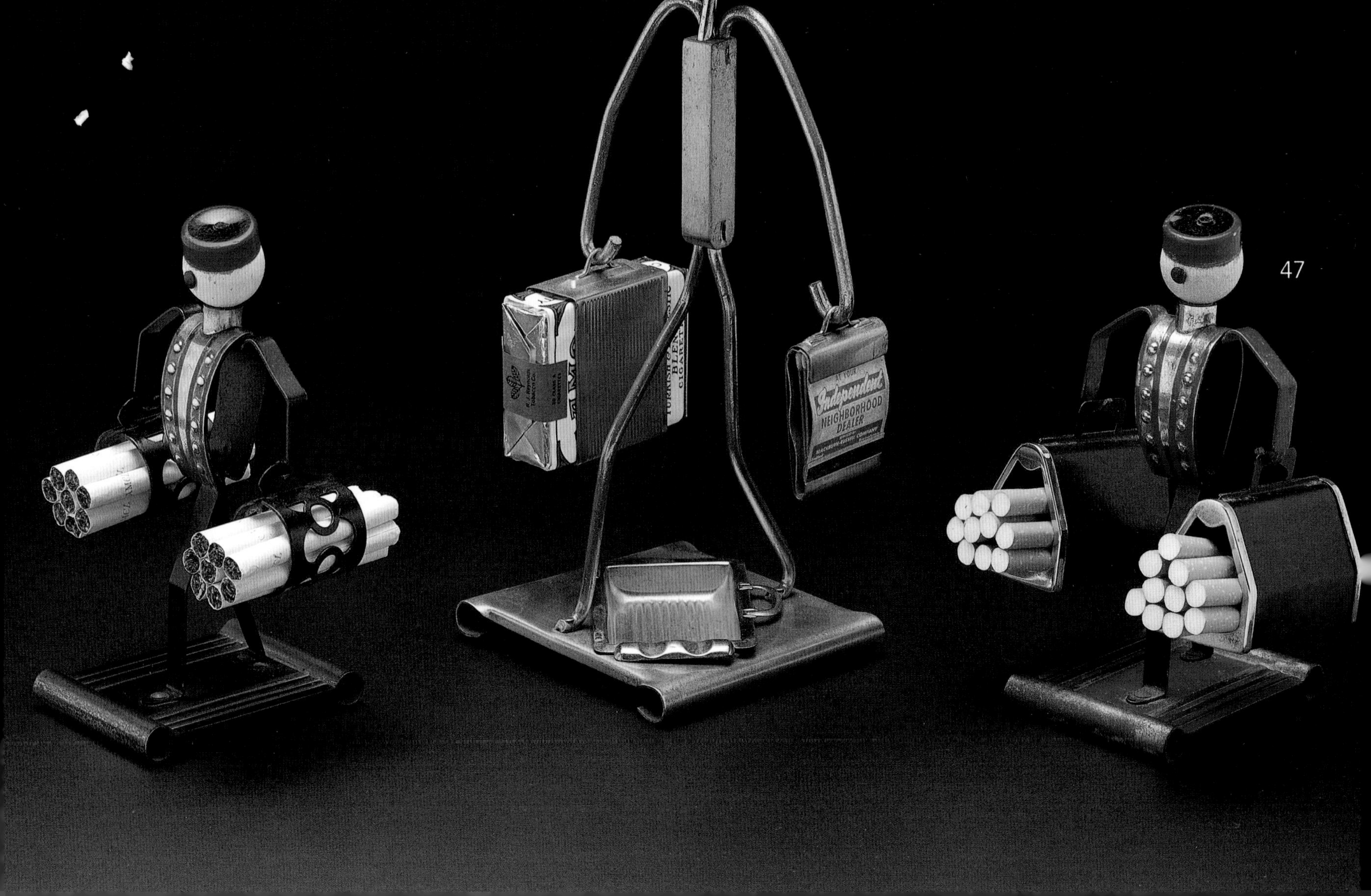

OUTSTANDING **graphic imagery** WOOED THE TOBACCO BUYER IN PRESS AND POSTER ADVERTISING. "PRINCE ALBERT" TOBACCO FROM R.J. REYNOLDS ADMIRABLY DEMONSTRATES SUCCESSFUL, SKILLFUL IMAGERY WITH A CUT-OUT DISPLAY CARD, C. 1910.

48

TAREYTONS ARE A QUARTER AGAIN

"The Dude" advertised
Herbert Tareyton
cigarettes for American
Brands through the
Depression years with
an up market image and
competitive price.

49

An elegant **iron smokestand**, manufactured in Belgium, measures 3 feet high with attached matchbox holder and table space for cocktails, cigarettes, and ashtray, c. 1929. *Noel Barrett Collection.*

An unusual and **rare gentleman's cane**, incorporating a custom-made Ronson De-Light lighter. The cane is horn tipped, black lacquered hickory, with a yellow wooden tip. The lighter, concealed in the cane behind a presentation engraved shield, is a modified, patented finger piece and snuffer cap by De-Light. U.S., 1929. *Dick Stettler Collection.*

Men's Bathrobes and Smoking Jackets

SINCE this catalog was printed, Men's Smoking Jackets and Blanket Robes have almost doubled in price. Inquiry in your own home town will demonstrate this. Once our catalog is printed we cannot change our prices; therefore, the man who orders from this page will get what is equivalent to almost two dollars for every dollar he pays.

33D3556 $3.49

Figured Blanket Cloth
33D3556 Men's Smoking Jacket or House Coat of a fine quality figured Blanket Cloth, in shawl collar style with two pockets, double cuffs and inside satin yoke. Collar, front cuffs and pockets are trimmed with cord; closes with silk frogs. All seams piped to insure good wear. Gray, navy blue, green or brown mixtures. Sizes, 34 to 44. State size and color.
Our price, each...... $3.49

33D3526 $4.98

33D970 $2.75

33D3506 $4.50

33D3550 $4.98

Wool Mixed Cheviot
Men's Smoking Jacket or House Coat, of very fine quality Wool Mixed Cheviot, shawl collar style, Oxford gray, blue or brown, trimmed with collar, pockets and cuffs of contrasting color. Silk cords and two novelty frog silk loops for closing. Sizes, 36 to 44. State size.
33D3550 Oxford.
33D3552 Blue.
33D3554 Brown.
Our price, each........ $4.98

33D3501 $3.69

Genuine Navajo Blanket
Navajo Blanket Robe in true Indian pattern and colorings. New York has no blanket more popular and it is in big demand at a price much higher than we ask. Cord at neck, heavy girdle and two pockets. Sizes, 34 to 46. State size.
33D3526 Blue and Gold.
33D3527 Gray and Red.
33D3528 Brown and Red.
Our price, each $4.98

Heavy Blanket Cloth
33D970 Boys' and Young Men's Bathrobes, of heavy weight Blanket Cloth. Cut extra full with lay-down collar; convenient pockets, tassel and cord at neck and girdle around the waist. Splendid shades of gray, blue and brown. This robe will give excellent service and you can depend upon it for long wear. A bargain at our price. Sizes, 6 to 16 years. State age and color.
Our price, each., $2.75

Handsome Designs
Men's Blanket Robe of good quality Blanketing, best shades and very handsome designs. Can be depended upon for wear and service. Has patch pockets, tassel at neck and heavy cord at waist. Sizes, 34 to 44. State age.
33D3501 Gray.
33D3504 Blue.
33D3505 Brown.
Our price, each $3.69

33D3532 $6.98

Slippers Free

Heavy Blanketing
Men's Semi-Shawl Collar Bathrobe of extra fine quality Blanketing in handsome color combinations. Made as pictured, the collar and pockets trimmed with silk cord. Has satin yoke in back. Sizes, 34 to 48 chest. State size.
33D3506 Blue and Tan.
33D3508 Brown and Blue.
33D3510 Oxford and Maroon.
Our price, each $4.50

Rich Colorings
Men's Extra Quality Blanket Robe, made as pictured; satin yoke inside. Sizes, 34 to 48. State size.
33D3520 Blue and Tan.
33D3522 Gray and Red.
33D3524 Navy Blue and Tan.
Our price, each $5.98

Slippers to Match
Blanket Robe and Slippers to match. A great bargain at the small price we ask. Robe is made as pictured and has satin yoke. The slippers match the robe. Great value at our price. Sizes, 34 to 48. State size.
33D3532 Green and Gold.
33D3534 Gray and Red.
33D3536 Green and Red.
Our price, Robe and Slippers.. $6.98

33D3520 $5.98

52

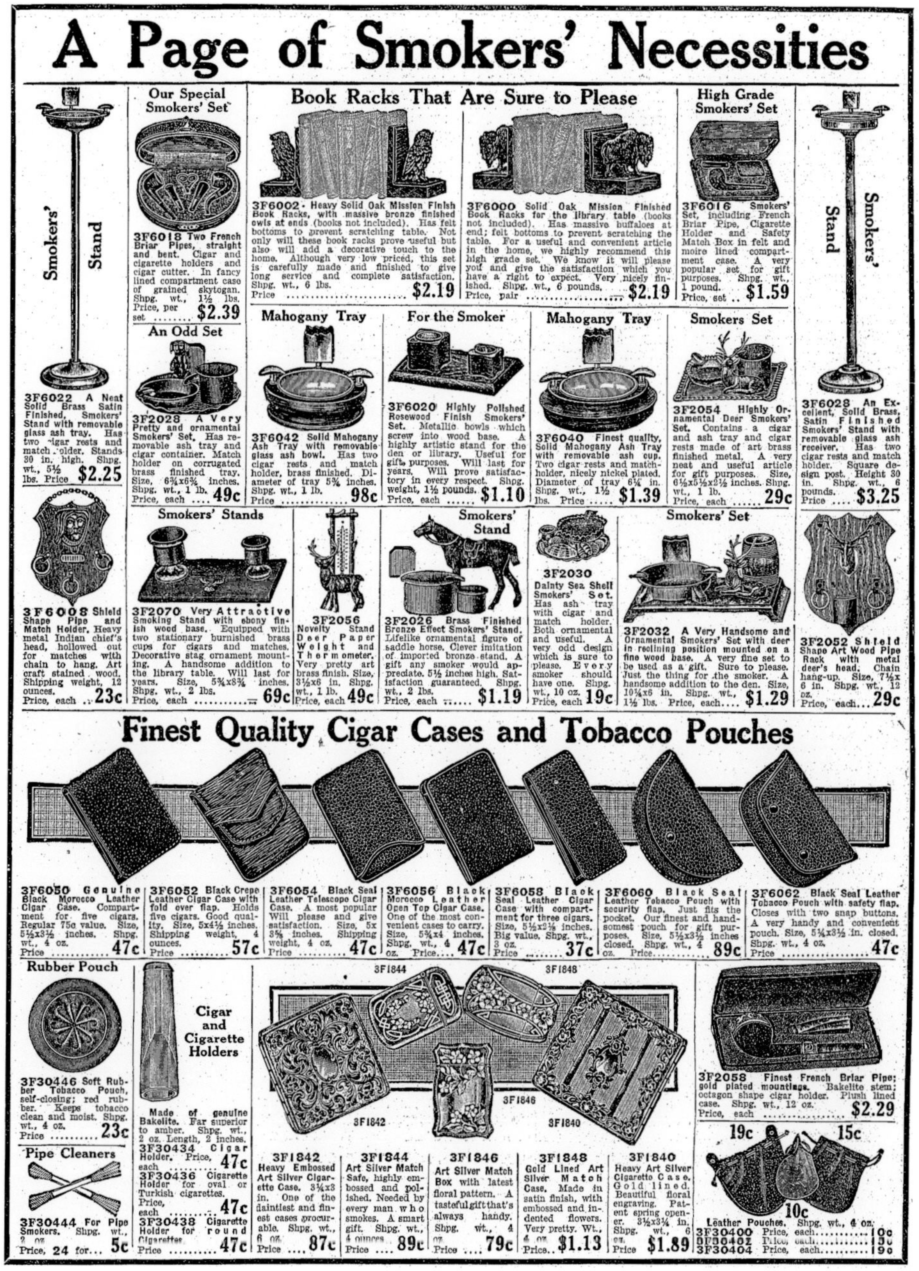

A Page of Smokers' Necessities

Smokers' Stand

3F6022 A Neat Solid Brass Satin Finished, Smokers' Stand with removable glass ash tray. Has two cigar rests and match holder. Stands 30 in. high. Shpg. wt., 5½ lbs. Price **$2.25**

Our Special Smokers' Set

3F6018 Two French Briar Pipes, straight and bent. Cigar and cigarette holders and cigar cutter. In fancy lined compartment case of grained skytogan. Shpg. wt., 1½ lbs. Price, per set **$2.39**

An Odd Set

3F2028 A Very Pretty and ornamental Smokers' Set. Has removable ash tray and cigar container. Match holder on corrugated brass finished tray. Size, 6¾x6¾ inches. Shpg. wt., 1 lb. Price, each **49c**

Book Racks That Are Sure to Please

3F6002 Heavy Solid Oak Mission Finish Book Racks, with massive bronze finished owls at ends (books not included). Has felt bottoms to prevent scratching table. Not only will these book racks prove useful but also will add a decorative touch to the home. Although very low priced, this set is carefully made and finished to give long service and complete satisfaction. Shpg. wt., 6 lbs. Price **$2.19**

3F6000 Solid Oak Mission Finished Book Racks for the library table (books not included). Has massive buffaloes at end; felt bottoms to prevent scratching the table. For a useful and convenient article in the home, we highly recommend this high grade set. We know it will please you and give the satisfaction which you have a right to expect. Very nicely finished. Shpg. wt., 6 pounds. Price, pair **$2.19**

High Grade Smokers' Set

3F6016 Smokers' Set, including French Briar Pipe, Cigarette Holder and Safety Match Box in felt and moire lined compartment case. A very popular set for gift purposes. Shpg. wt., 1 pound. Price, set .. **$1.59**

Mahogany Tray

3F6042 Solid Mahogany Ash Tray with removable glass ash bowl. Has two cigar rests and match holder, brass finished. Diameter of tray 5¾ inches. Shpg. wt., 1 lb. Price **98c**

For the Smoker

3F6020 Highly Polished Rosewood Finish Smokers' Set. Metallic bowls which screw into wood base. A highly artistic stand for the den or library. Useful for gift purposes. Will last for years. Will prove satisfactory in every respect. Shpg. weight, 1½ pounds. Price, each **$1.10**

Mahogany Tray

3F6040 Finest quality, Solid Mahogany Ash Tray with removable ash cup. Two cigar rests and matchholder, nicely nickel plated. Diameter of tray 6¼ in. Shpg. wt., 1½ lbs. Price **$1.39**

Smokers Set

3F2054 Highly Ornamental Deer Smokers' Set. Contains a cigar and ash tray and cigar rests made of art brass finished metal. A very neat and useful article for gift purposes. Size, 6½x5½x2½ inches. Shpg. wt., 1 lb. Price, each **29c**

Smokers' Stand

3F6028 An Excellent, Solid Brass, Satin Finished Smokers' Stand with removable glass ash receiver. Has two cigar rests and match holder. Square design post. Height 30 in. Shpg. wt., 6 pounds. Price **$3.25**

3F6008 Shield Shape Pipe and Match Holder. Heavy metal Indian chief's head, hollowed out for matches with chain to hang. Art craft stained wood. Shipping weight, 12 ounces. Price, each .. **23c**

Smokers' Stands

3F2070 Very Attractive Smoking Stand with ebony finish wood base. Equipped with two stationary burnished brass cups for cigars and matches. Decorative stag ornament mounting. A handsome addition to the library table. Will last for years. Size, 5¾x8¾ inches. Shpg. wt., 2 lbs. Price, each **69c**

3F2056 Novelty Stand Deer Paper Weight and Thermometer. Very pretty art brass finish. Size, 3½x6 in. Shpg. wt., 1 lb. Price, each **49c**

Smokers' Stand

3F2026 Brass Finished Bronze Effect Smokers' Stand. Lifelike ornamental figure of saddle horse. Clever imitation of imported bronze stand. A gift any smoker would appreciate. 5½ inches high. Satisfaction guaranteed. Shpg. wt., 2 lbs. Price, each **$1.19**

3F2030 Dainty Sea Shell Smokers' Set. Has ash tray with cigar and match holder. Both ornamental and useful. A very odd design which is sure to please. Every smoker should have one. Shpg. wt., 10 oz. Price, each **19c**

Smokers' Set

3F2032 A Very Handsome and Ornamental Smokers' Set with deer in reclining position mounted on a fine wood base. A very fine set to be used as a gift. Sure to please. Just the thing for the smoker. A handsome addition to the den. Size, 10¼x6 in. Shpg. wt., 1½ lbs. Price, each.... **$1.29**

3F2052 Shield Shape Art Wood Pipe Rack with metal deer's head. Chain hang-up. Size, 7½x6 in. Shpg. wt., 12 oz. Price, each... **29c**

Finest Quality Cigar Cases and Tobacco Pouches

3F6050 Genuine Black Morocco Leather Cigar Case. Compartment for five cigars. Regular 75c value. Size, 5½x3½ inches. Shpg. wt., 4 oz. Price **47c**

3F6052 Black Crepe Leather Cigar Case with fold over flap. Holds five cigars. Good quality. Size, 5x4½ inches. Shipping weight, 4 ounces. Price **57c**

3F6054 Black Seal Leather Telescope Cigar Case. A most popular Will please and give satisfaction. Size, 5x3⅝ inches. Shipping weight, 4 oz. Price **47c**

3F6056 Black Morocco Leather Open Top Cigar Case. One of the most convenient cases to carry. Size, 5¾x4 inches. Shpg. wt., 4 oz. Price.... **47c**

3F6058 Black Seal Leather Cigar Case with compartment for three cigars. Size, 5½x2⅛ inches. Big value. Shpg. wt., 3 oz. Price **37c**

3F6060 Black Seal Leather Tobacco Pouch with security flap. Just fits the pocket. Our finest and handsomest pouch for gift purposes. Size, 5½x3½ inches closed. Shpg. wt., 4 oz. Price........... **89c**

3F6062 Black Seal Leather Tobacco Pouch with safety flap. Closes with two snap buttons. A very handy and convenient pouch. Size, 5¼x3½ in. closed. Shpg. wt., 4 oz. Price **47c**

Rubber Pouch

3F30446 Soft Rubber Tobacco Pouch, self-closing; red rubber. Keeps tobacco clean and moist. Shpg. wt., 4 oz. Price **23c**

Pipe Cleaners

3F30444 For Pipe Smokers. Shpg. wt., 2 oz. Price, 24 for... **5c**

Cigar and Cigarette Holders

Made of genuine Bakelite. Far superior to amber. Shpg. wt., 2 oz. Length, 2 inches.

3F30434 Cigar Holder. Price, each **47c**

3F30436 Cigarette Holder for oval or Turkish cigarettes. Price, each **47c**

3F30438 Cigarette Holder for round Cigarettes. Price **47c**

3F1844 3F1848 3F1846 3F1842 3F1840

3F1842 Heavy Embossed Art Silver Cigarette Case. 3¼x3 in. One of the daintiest and finest cases procurable. Shpg. wt., 6 oz. Price **87c**

3F1844 Art Silver Match Safe, highly embossed and polished. Needed by every man who smokes. A smart gift. Shpg. wt., 4 ounces. Price **89c**

3F1846 Art Silver Match Box with latest floral pattern. A tasteful gift that's always handy. Shpg. wt., 4 oz. Price **79c**

3F1848 Gold Lined Art Silver Match Case. Made in satin finish, with embossed and indented flowers. Very pretty. Wt., 4 oz. Price.. **$1.13**

3F1840 Heavy Art Silver Cigarette Case. Gold lined. Beautiful floral engraving. Patent spring opener. 3½x3¼ in. Shpg. wt., 6 oz. Price **$1.89**

3F2058 Finest French Briar Pipe; gold plated mountings. Bakelite stem; octagon shape cigar holder. Plush lined case. Shpg. wt., 12 oz. Price, each **$2.29**

19c 15c 10c

Leather Pouches. Shpg. wt., 4 oz.

3F30400 Price, each........... 10c
3F30402 Price, each........... 15c
3F30404 Price, each........... 19c

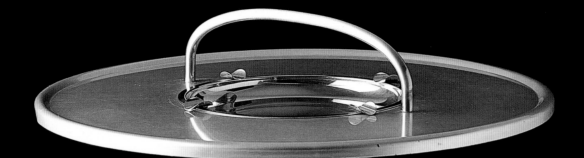

54

A PATENTED DESIGN BY FUNDERBURK ENGINEERING, WALTHAM, MASSACHUSETTS. THE **chrome and metal ashtray** TABLE AREA IS SUPPORTED BY THREE CONCENTRIC COBALT BLUE GLASS RODS, c. 1934. *COURTESY: HARVEY'S, MELROSE AVENUE.*

AN **Art Deco side table** WITH ARTICULATING ASHTRAY AND MATCH HOLDER. THE HEIGHT OF THE ASHTRAY CAN BE ADJUSTED, AND ITS ATTACHMENT ALLOWS A 360 DEGREE SWIVEL. CHROME AND PAINTED METAL WITH BAKELITE TRIM. *COURTESY: HARVEY'S, MELROSE AVENUE.*

AN **ashstand** DESIGNED BY
WOLFGANG HOFFMANN, C. 1934.
DESIGNED FOR CHAIRSIDE OR LOUNGE USE,
THE GLASS TABLE AREA ACCOMMODATES
CIGARETTES, LIGHTER, AND COCKTAILS.
COURTESY: PICCOLO PETE'S, SHERMAN OAKS.

A **Gentleman's Companion, or
Smoker's Companion.** THIS EXAMPLE FROM
BELGIUM IN CHROME AND BLACK BAKELITE FEATURES
A SMALL TABLE AREA FOR CHAIRSIDE LEISURE
CONVENIENCE, TWENTY-EIGHT INCHES HIGH. MANY
VARIATIONS OF THIS DESIGN WERE PRODUCED
THROUGH THE TWENTIES AND THIRTIES.
AUTHOR COLLECTION.

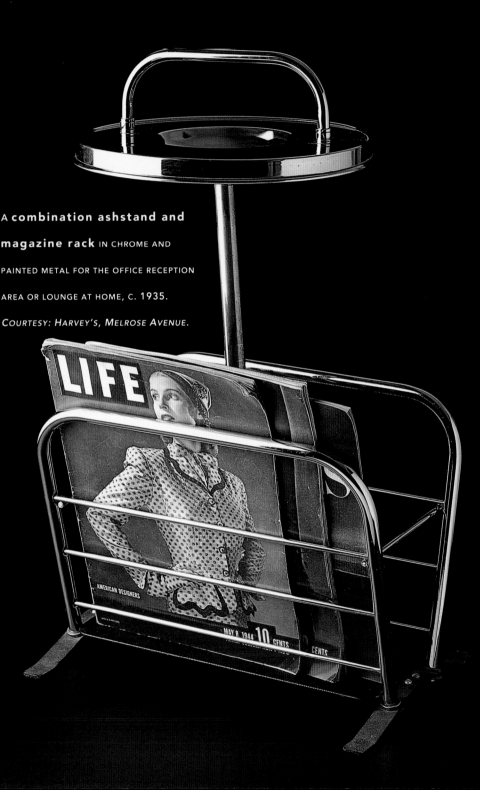

A **combination ashstand and magazine rack** IN CHROME AND PAINTED METAL FOR THE OFFICE RECEPTION AREA OR LOUNGE AT HOME, C. 1935.
COURTESY: HARVEY'S, MELROSE AVENUE.

AN ENORMOUS VARIETY OF SILKS IMAGES WAS OFFERED, ALONG WITH INSTRUCTIONS FROM THE PLAYER TOBACCO COMPANY: ¶ "THE SATIN INSERTS MAY BE STITCHED (HERRINGBONE STYLE) ON A PIECE OF SILK, SATIN OR OTHER MATERIAL. AS INDICATED SOME SIMPLE EMBROIDERY ADDS GREATLY TO THE ATTRACTIVENESS OF THE FINISHED ARTICLE. OTHER THINGS WHICH CAN BE MADE OF THE INSERT ARE SCREENS, BEDSPREADS, LAMP SHADES, SEWING BAGS, HAT BANDS, PORTIERES, PIN CUSHIONS, DOILIES, TABLE CENTERS, MASQUERADE DRESSES, BELTS, BANDS FOR THE HAIR, KIMONOS, PILLOW TOPS, TIES, PIANO DRAPES, TABLECLOTHS, DOLL'S DRESSES, TEAPOT COSIES, EGG COSIES, MANTEL DRAPES, COMFORTERS, HANDKERCHIEF BAGS, SIDEBOARD COVERS, DRESSER COVERS, COVERS FOR CHAIRS, PARASOLS, ETC. ¶ A COLORED SHEET SHOWING SOME OF THE USES TO WHICH THESE INSERTS MAY BE PUT WILL BE MAILED TO YOU POST FREE ON RECEIPT OF YOUR NAME AND POSTAL ADDRESS."
CLETUS WRIGHT COLLECTION.

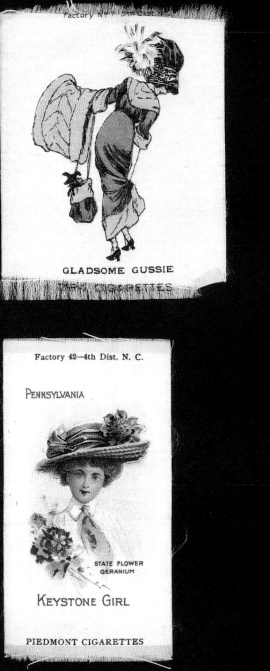

Factory Ne...

GLADSOME GUSSIE

...CIGARETTES

ZIRA CIGARETTES

"Don't You Tell!"

Factory No. 7, 5th Dist. N.J.

ZIRA GIRLS
THE SMILE CLOAKERS

ESTELLE

ROSE – RUN ESTELLE, RUN! THOSE
MEN ARE ZIRA SMOKERS

ZIRA CIGARETTES

Factory 42—4th Dist. N. C.

PENNSYLVANIA

STATE FLOWER
GERANIUM

KEYSTONE GIRL

PIEDMONT CIGARETTES

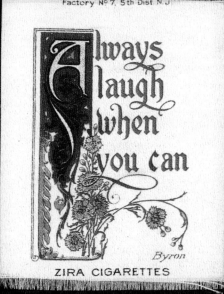

Factory Nº 7, 5th Dist. N.J.

Always
I laugh
when
you can

Byron

ZIRA CIGARETTES

MOGUL CIGARETTE

Andrew Johnson

1865–1869

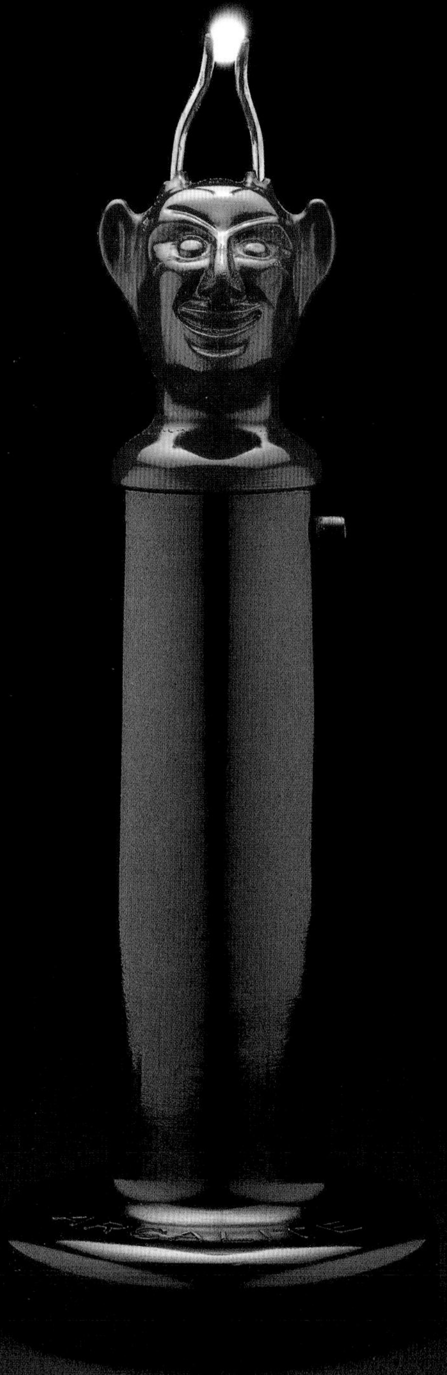

58

MANUFACTURED IN PHILADELPHIA

BY ARCALITE, THIS CURIOUS

electric table lighter

IN BLACK AND MAROON BAKELITE

IS ELECTRICALLY OPERATED.

WHEN THE BUTTON IS

DEPRESSED, A SPARK JUMPS

ACROSS THE TIPS OF THE DEVIL'S

TWO COPPER HORNS.

A RARE ODDITY, C. 1928.

DICK STETTLER COLLECTION.

BOOK MATCHES WERE POPULAR TO CARRY MESSAGES OF EVERY DESCRIPTION. PRIMARILY A GIVE-AWAY, MATCHES ADVERTISED HOTELS, BARS, CONSUMER PRODUCTS, POLITICAL CAMPAIGNS, CONVENTIONS, EXPOSITIONS, ENTERTAINMENT, FILMS, AND ALL MANNER OF SPECIAL EVENTS. THEY WERE THE FORERUNNER OF THE T-SHIRT AND BUMPER STICKER. DURING WORLD WAR II, PROPAGANDA WRITERS PRODUCED SOME UNFORGETTABLE ADVERTISING SLOGANS AND GRAPHICS: "MAKE IT HOT FOR HITLER" AND "STRIKE 'EM DEAD" ADMIRABLY FIT THIS CATEGORY. THE "STRIKE 'EM DEAD" MATCHES CONTAINED AN ARMY OF ADOLF MATCHES, AT ATTENTION, WAITING TO BE "STRUCK DEAD."

MANUFACTURED BY LION MATCH CO., SAN FRANCISCO, CA. AUTHOR COLLECTION.

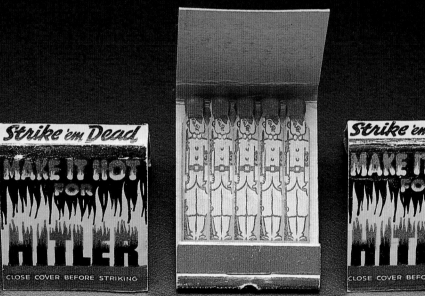

FRIVOLITY HAS OFTEN BEEN THE
PREROGATIVE OF **book match
purveyors**. WHAT CONFUCIUS SAYS
ACCORDING TO THIS MATCHBOOK IS BEST
OMITTED. IT IS DOUBTFUL WHETHER THIS
PARTICULAR QUOTE COULD BE
AUTHENTICATED IN HISTORICAL TEXTS.
*MANUFACTURED IN ENGLAND BY BOURNE
OF HARLESDON LTD., C. 1966.*
AUTHOR COLLECTION.

60

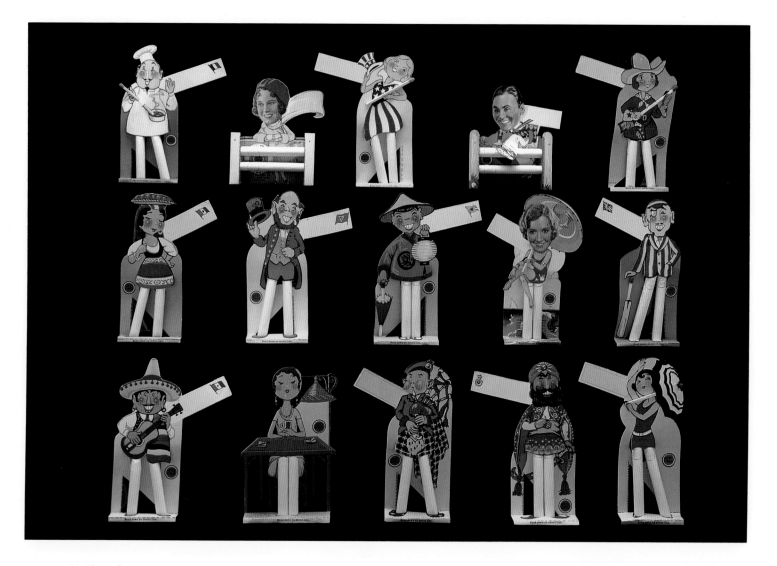

Bridge favors and place cards WERE "OFFERED IN ORDER TO CALL ATTENTION TO THE MERITS OF **LUCKY STRIKE** CIGARETTES," IN THE EARLY THIRTIES. TOP ROW FEATURES GINGER ROGERS (SECOND LEFT), AND EDDIE BUZZELL, "A COLUMBIA STAR" (SECOND RIGHT). CENTER ROW FEATURES ONA MUNSON, "A FIRST NATIONAL STAR," AND MARRIED TO BUZZELL AT THE TIME (SECOND LEFT). CUT OUT SPACES WERE PROVIDED FOR THE INSERTION OF CIGARETTES TO COMPLETE THE ILLUSTRATIONS. *CLETUS WRIGHT COLLECTION.*

A MID-THIRTIES EXAMPLE OF THE

chromed-metal smokestands

THAT ENJOYED GREAT POPULARITY. THE

VARIED DESIGNS INCORPORATED

COMPONENTS OF AN ELECTRIC LIGHTER,

AN ASHTRAY, AND A TOBACCO HUMIDOR OR

CIGARETTE HOLDER. THE COMMON DESIGN

ELEMENT WAS AN ILLUMINATED GLASS BASE

AND, SOMETIMES, ILLUMINATED MOTIFS

PROVIDING AN ATTRACTIVE STATEMENT IN

THE SMOKER'S LOUNGE OR PARLOR. THIS

MODEL SPORTS A PASSENGER AIRCRAFT

WITH COCKPIT AND INTERIOR ILLUMINATION,

PROBABLY MANUFACTURED IN CANADA.

COURTESY: PICCOLO PETE'S,

SHERMAN OAKS.

62

THIS 1932 **RCA radio** REFLECTED THE ORIGINAL WINGS CIGARETTE PACK DESIGN IN EVERY DETAIL. ANOTHER MODEL IN PAINTED METAL OVER A WOOD CABINET SPORTED SIDE CONTROLS, COMPLETING A LARGE FACSIMILE OF THE FAMOUS PACK. INTRODUCED IN 1930, THE PACK WAS REDUCED IN PRICE BY THE MANUFACTURERS, BROWN & WILLIAMSON, IN 1932 TO 10 CENTS PER PACK, MAKING IT THE FIRST U.S. ECONOMY-PRICED CIGARETTE. *JOE KOESTER COLLECTION.*

A PRESENTATION **gas table lighter**, c. 1968, MANUFACTURED IN JAPAN BY BRONICA.

DICK STETTLER COLLECTION.

A **chromed metal "bomb" lighter and painted metal ashtray** MANUFACTURED IN THE U.S., C. 1935. THE WHEEL AND FLINT ACTION LIGHTER CAN BE REMOVED FROM ITS MOUNT TO FACILITATE USE. *DICK STETTLER COLLECTION.*

65

MANY AIRCRAFT WERE COPIED IN STYLIZED FASHION ON cigarette lighters. A NEGBAUR FROM GERMANY, C. 1948, FEATURES AN AUTOMATIC OPENER THAT IS ACTIVATED BY TURNING THE PROPELLER OF THE P-51 MUSTANG (LEFT). THE AUSTRIAN-MADE BENTLEY IS A STYLIZED F-86D, C. 1958 (CENTER), AND THE F-102 IS MANUFACTURED BY SAROME, JAPAN (RIGHT). DICK STETTLER COLLECTION.

A **pewter souvenir ashtray** EMBOSSED WITH "B-29 SUPERFORTRESS" UNDER AN ILLUSTRATION OF THE

FAMOUS WORLD WAR II BOMBER. COURTESY: OFF THE WALL, LOS ANGELES.

THIS FAITHFUL REPRODUCTION OF THE JOHNSON'S WAX RESEARCH TOWER IN RACINE, WISCONSIN, DESIGNED BY FRANK LLOYD WRIGHT, IS APPROXIMATELY 7 INCHES HIGH AND UTILIZES A FLINT AND WHEEL MECHANISM. IT IS A UNIQUE **table lighter** IN CHROMED METAL. *HARVEY SCHWARTZ COLLECTION.*

Small table lighters, REMINISCENT OF LIPSTICKS, WERE ACCEPTABLE ON THE DRESSING TABLE AS A DECORATIVE AND FUNCTIONAL ACCESSORY. SEVERAL ARE OF U.S. MANUFACTURE, IN BAKELITE AND LUCITE (A, E, F, AND G). POCKET LIGHTERS FROM REGENS SPORT ENAMELLED ART DECO MOTIFS ON CHROME PLATED METAL, C. 1930 (B, C, AND D). A CLASSIC ART DECO MOTIF ADORNS A GOLDEN WHEEL AUTOMATIC; GREEN, RED, AND BLACK ENAMELLING ON BRASS, C. 1930 (K). PROBABLY THE MOST COMMON RONSON POCKET LIGHTER, THIS MODEL WAS MADE IN ENGLAND IN THE LATE FORTIES AND ENJOYED MANY YEARS OF PRODUCTION (J). IT WAS BLATANTLY COPIED BY FOREIGN AND DOMESTIC COMPETITORS SUCH AS THE MODEL FROM PARTNER FEATURING GRAPHICS OF NEW YORK CITY LANDMARKS (L). ¶ THE FIRST POCKET LIGHTERS PRODUCED BY A U.S. MANUFACTURER, THESE EVANS COMPANY MODELS ARE ILLUSTRATED IN TWO COLOR COMBINATIONS (H AND M). BOTH HAVE ENAMELLED MOTIFS ON SILVER PLATE, AND THE MECHANISM IS LIFT-ARM, WHEEL AND FLINT, USING PETROL. "SOUVENIR OF HOLLAND" AND "QUEEN OF NEW WESTMINSTER" ARE SIMILAR DESIGNS, MADE IN JAPAN BY SWG AND E.A. MORRIS, RESPECTIVELY (O AND R). THESE WERE MARKETED AS KEYRING LIGHTERS, AS WERE THE "S.S. SANTA ROSA" (Q); A "SAROME CRUISER" FROM SEGAWA, ADVERTISED AS AN "AUTOMATIC SUPER LIGHTER"; AND THE SAROME "BLUE BIRD" CAR, PRODUCED IN JAPAN, C. 1965 (P). ALL USED FLINT AND WHEEL MECHANISMS. THESE INEXPENSIVE IMPORTS CREATED POTENT COMPETITION FOR U.S. SUPPLIERS IN THE SIXTIES. *JUNE BERLINER COLLECTION, (A–H, K, M–R). AUTHOR COLLECTION, (J). KAY TORNBORG COLLECTION, (L).*

A **West German-made Jeep lighter/cigarette box** WITH ASHTRAY TENDER, IN STAINLESS STEEL, C. 1951 (LEFT). THE LIGHTER MECHANISM IS CONCEALED IN THE HOOD. THE **Harley Davidson lighter** WITH BUTANE GAS FUEL STARTED PRODUCTION IN JAPAN IN THE SEVENTIES AND CONTINUES. *DICK STETTLER COLLECTION.*

70

A VERY RARE **Ronson "Pist-o-Liter" sparker** FOR LIGHTING LANTERNS, GAS APPLIANCES, AND TINDER FOR CIGARETTES, 1910.

PERRY GROVER COLLECTION.

71

THE DETONATOR HANDLE, WHEN DEPRESSED, CAUSES THE

FLAME TO APPEAR FROM THIS **spark-action butane**

lighter, MANUFACTURED IN JAPAN BY PIEZO

ELECTRONIC, c. 1972. DICK STETTLER COLLECTION.

A **ship's wheel**
cigarette lighter IN BRASS,
MADE IN THE EARLY THIRTIES,
SPAWNED MANY COPIES.
MANUFACTURER UNKNOWN.
DICK STETTLER COLLECTION.

72

74

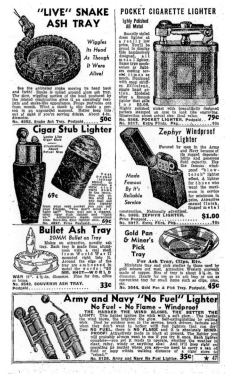

"LIVE" SNAKE ASH TRAY

Wiggles Its Head As Though It Were Alive!

See the animated snake moving its head back and forth! Snake is coiled around glass ash tray. The slow, wiggling motion of the head produced by the jointed construction gives it an amazingly realistic and snake-like appearance. Fangs protrude out from mouth. What a shock to slip beside a person in an unguarded moment. Either keep this out of sight if you're serving drinks. About 4-in. diameter.
No. 4952. Snake Ash Tray. Postpaid.... **50c**

POCKET CIGARETTE LIGHTER

Highly Polished All Metal

Smartly styled dress lighter at a really low price. You'll be proud to display this handsomely designed, all metal lighter. Same type mechanism as light-em costing several times as much. Equipped with snap muffler. Efficient, single hand action. Modeled after a famous lighter that sells for $5.00. Highly polished nickel with beautifully designed pattern stamped on case to look like engraving. Illustration about actual size. Real value.
No. 9368. POCKET LIGHTER. Postpaid.... **79c**
No. 9317. Extra Flints. Pkg.......... **10c**

Cigar Stub Lighter

Looks Like Cigar Stub
Illustration About Actual Size

Vest pocket lighter styled to resemble a cigar stub right down to the moist tan ash on the end. As you pull out this lighter from your vest pocket, your friends "You don't need a cigarette." Then, pull out a cigarette "now stub lighter and "light up!" Attractively made, convenient and useful. Sure-fire flint lighter unit.
No. 4827. Price Postpaid.......... **69c**

Bullet Ash Tray

20MM Bullet on Tray

Makes an attractive, novelty ash tray. Each tray is made from aluminum with a real shell from World War II mounted right into it. Around the edge of the tray are embossed in metal the words: "20 MM, SHOT—WORLD WAR II", 4½-in. diameter. Fine for den, office or home.
No. 3542. SOUVENIR ASH TRAY. Postpaid.......... **33c**

Zephyr Windproof Lighter

Favored by men in the Army and Navy because of its rugged dependability and generous fluid capacity. Has the famous windproof "blow-torch" lighter effect. A lighter for those who want the maximum in service for minimum in price. Attractive enamel finish. Rugged metal construction. Nationally advertised.
No. 9368. ZEPHYR LIGHTER. Price Postpaid.... **$1.00**
No. 9317. Extra Flint. Pkg.......... **10c**

Gold Pan & Miner's Pick Tray

For Ash Tray, Clips, Etc.

Miniature pan and pick similar to those used by gold miners out west. Attractive Western souvenir made of copper. Size of tray is about 3¼-in. in diameter. Handy for use as an ash tray or use as convenient tray for small items such as clips, pins, etc.
No. 3544. Gold Pan & Pick Tray. Postpaid.... **45c**

Army and Navy "No Fuel" Lighter

No Fuel - No Flame - Windproof

THE HARDER THE WIND BLOWS, THE BETTER THE LIGHT! This lighter ignites the wick with a soft glow. The harder the wind blows, the brighter the glow. Self-extinguishing by pulling wick. Used by outdoor men in the service, truck drivers, farmers and when they don't want to bother with fuel lighters that run dry! Uses NO FUEL, there is NO FLAME and it is absolutely WINDPROOF! Attractively made in black at present. The lighter you will probably always want to use if you try it once. Each lighter complete—you get it ready to operate, whether the weather is clear, rainy, windy or anything else! And it'll keep right on operating no matter where you are—no need to carry a can of fluid or keep within walking distance of a cigar store to "reload."
No. 6126. Army and Navy No Fuel Lighter. **35c** ★ 47

Arrowhead Ash Tray

WESTWARD HO! Out of the West comes this souvenir ash tray. Looks smart in your office, den or room. Genuine copper with oxidized finish. Hand painted Indian or Western design on tray. About 3½-in. long, 4-in. wide.
No. 3585. Arrowhead Ash Tray. Postpaid.... **39c**

Cowboy Hat Ash Tray

Most popular ash tray souvenir from the West. These are made in the cow country out of pure copper. Look smart and serve a useful purpose. Can be used as an ash tray, for pins, as paper weight, etc. 3-in. diameter.
No. 3586. Cowboy Hat Ash Tray. Postpaid.... **25c**

Fireplace Ash Tray

Made in the form of fireplace out of composition material. Place for cigarettes on one side and matches on other side. In center is grate cigarette rest. Ashes fall through grate into tray. Convenient, practical. Smoke goes up chimney. Fascinating. Large size. 5x4x4-in. Realistically colored.
No. 3587. Fireplace Ash Tray. Postpaid.... **$2.95**

LUMINOUS ASH TRAY

Useful for Smoking in Dark

A practical ash tray that you can use in the dark with safety. Up till now, smoking in the dark has been a fire hazard. In theaters, shows, darkly lit rooms, at night in bed, for watchmen, in dark rooms, etc. it serves a practical and useful purpose. About 4-in. diameter.
No. 3588. Luminous Ash Tray. Postpaid.... **89c**

Comic Ash Tray

Makes an Interesting Bridge Gift or Prize

A novel ash tray that will prove very popular with your friends. Always good for a laugh. Each tray is made of crystal-like glass, attractively designed in hexagonal shape, (inlaid under glass in bottom is a colorful scene with the inscription "Put Your Butts Here." Can be used as a novel gift or prize and seldom fails to provide amusement.
No. 3589. Comic Ash Tray. Price Postpaid.... **49c**

Flints and Wick for Lighters

An Extra Supply Ready

If you have a cigarette lighter, you should secure a package of extra flints with extra wick. Bright spark, quicker light.
No. 9317. Flints and Wick. Package.... **10c**

Jugo Pencil Lighter

"Handiest" Lighter that is Made!

Not Just a Gadget But a Reliable Lighter and Dependable Mechanical Pencil. No Larger Than Regular Pencil.

Here is the most amazing development in the history of either Pencils or Lighters. All the best features of the finest, have been combined in "JUGO," the precision built Pencil Lighter. Handsomely styled by expert craftsmen, this smart looking combination comes in a convenient size for den and women. Two distinctive, gleaming color combinations of black with gold plating or black with silver plating.

Precision Built---Handsomely Styled

The Pencil, with extra leads and eraser, is the most efficient mechanical type ever developed. The Lighter is a midget fuel-mixer with everlasting wick, and extra flints. Packed in individual acetate containers makes it ideal for a gift. JUGO is a compliment to any pocket or purse! Since it takes up no more room than an ordinary mechanical pencil, you will enjoy its carrying convenience. The lighter that is right at your fingertips—the "handiest" lighter ever made. Standard pencil size, 5¼-in. long. With pocket clip.
No. 9407. JUGO PENCIL LIGHTER. Price Postpaid.... **$3.49**

EASY TO CARRY---EASY TO USE

SPECIAL NOTE. When ordering, be sure to give name of article as well as the stock number.
| Johnson Smith & Co., ★ Detroit, Mich. ★ 51

Filter Tip For Safer Smoking

20 FILTER TIP CIGARETTES 6¢

Make 20 Cigarettes in 5 Minutes
SaveMoney; Make Your Own Cigarettes

With this Spee-Dee Cigarette Maker it is easy to make your own cigarettes. Tobacco can be made whichever way you prefer. Use your own tobacco; use granulated, mentholated, Turkish or domestic tobacco, etc. There is no trouble making cigarettes as the machine does all the work. You put the tobacco in the tube, turn the handle and the cigarette is made. You should easily make 20 cigarettes in 5 minutes. Constructed entirely of metal. Insert paper tube, turn handle and cigarette is made. Height 5½ inches. Weight 5 ounces.
No. 4592. CIGARETTE MAKER. Price Postpaid.... **$1.98**
No. 4593. 100 TUBES TO MAKE 100 CIGARETTES. High grade French rice paper with built in filter tip. Price Postpaid Per 100.... **19c**
No. 4001A. 100 Plain Tubes to Make 100 Regular Cigarettes Without Filter Tip. Price Postpaid.... **15c**

"Comical" Cigaret Dispenser

Nod the Head...
Up Goes the Tail...
Out Comes Cigaret

The latest LAUGH PRODUCER! A nod of the head and out comes a cigaret... under the tail! In appearance it is a novel cigaret holder that is easily loaded with 20 cigarettes. Wood construction with movable head and tail. Design shows Old Hill Billy Mose sitting on the Jackass with a case of corn likker. Donkey stands upright in base waiting (almost begging) for someone to nod his head so that he can deliver another cigaret. The base is a colorful green. Jackass is in natural wood color with black and yellow markings. A suitable novelty for a man's office or den. Gets your party off to a flying start! Over 7½ inches high! Each in box. Makes an inexpensive prize or gift.
No. 8239. Jackass Cigaret Dispenser. Price Postpaid.... **75c**

THE PRIVY PIPE

Wind Proof!

A pipe for real men! The funniest pipe ever—yet it is a fine smoker and has some real advantages over other pipes, too. Although it is made in form of a toilet bowl, it is a good smoking pipe. The hinged lid makes it windproof and protects you from blowing ashes. Handsome briar finish. Hard bit. Good for plenty of laughs and a fine smoke. Full size. No breaking in.
No. 3406. The Privy Pipe.... **69c**

Paleface Luck Pouch

Paleface "Thunderbird" Luck Pouch

When you wear this charm, go close to the only morning to a place where you can see far to the south, east, sun and west. Execute a portion of this medicine to the four winds. Then face the rising sun and repeat this prayer, "Oh mighty one, fulfill my desire." If your medicine is strong, the "Thunderbird" will bring you your happiness and success.

Novelty and souvenir Pouch made of buckskin, Indian style. Filled with pipe needles.
No. 4696. Price Postpaid.... **35c**

Novelty Cigarette Dispenser & Ash Tray

Pull the Chain & Out Comes a Cigarette

Roars of Laughter Every Time It Goes Into Action! As a prize or unique gift it would be difficult to surpass. Starts any party off with a bang.

For parties—in the home—in the den—or just for fun! A combination attractive and useful combination cigarette dispenser and ash tray. Remove top cover, place cigarettes in box, pull string and a cigarette pops out of the side. The bowl is used as an ash tray. Ash tray bowl is removable and washable. Size about 10-in. high, 8¼-in. deep and 4-in. wide. Each in individual box.
No. 6610. Cigarette Dispenser & Ash Tray. Price Postpaid.... **$2.50**

Johnson Smith & Co., ★ 53

75

AN ORIGINAL **Eclair lighter** FROM FRANCE, C. 1933 (LEFT), WITH A REPRODUCTION **"Daltis" lighter**, C. 1960.

DICK STETTLER COLLECTION.

76

AN ELEGANT **standing ashstand**

IN CHROME AND ENAMELLED METAL, C. 1938.

COURTESY: HARVEY'S, MELROSE AVENUE.

78

A LEVER AT THE REAR OF THE TRAPEZOID

RELEASES A TRAP DOOR AT THE BIRD'S FEET.

THE BIRD DIPS TO RETRIEVE A CIGARETTE

AND THEN ASSUMES ITS ORIGINAL STANCE,

CIGARETTE IN BEAK, AS THE TRAP DOOR

CLOSES. ARTS AND CRAFTS DESIGN IN

COPPER AND BRASS WITH PORCELAIN INLAY.

ENGLISH **cigarette retriever**,

1909. *THOMAS A. GRAY COLLECTION.*

THE DELIGHTFUL **Ronson penguin "Pik-a-Cig" lighter and dispenser** COMBINATION IN PAINTED METAL AND CHROME DATES FROM 1930.

HORIZONTAL MOTION OF THE FRONT LEVER DISPENSES A CIGARETTE TO THE BASE OF THE BOX, WHICH IS THEN RETRIEVED AND HELD BY THE PENGUIN. U.S., WITH ART

METAL WORKS WHEEL AND FLINT LIGHTER. *JUNE BERLINER COLLECTION.*

AN EARLY FIFTIES **Japanese novelty lighter**, MANUFACTURER UNKNOWN. THE MECHANISM IS CONTAINED IN THE FLAT BASE OF THE BIRDCAGE. *DICK STETTLER COLLECTION.*

A **Japanese novelty lighter**, C. 1950. THE BIRD TILTS TO AN UPRIGHT, CHIRPING POSITION AND AN ILLUMINATED BEAK OFFERS A MODEST FLAME PRODUCED WHEN PRESSURE IS APPLIED TO THE TAIL. *DICK STETTLER COLLECTION.*

MANUFACTURED BETWEEN 1925 AND 1930, PROBABLY IN CHINA, THIS **wooden dispenser** WAS PRODUCED IN MANY FORMS. AS THE LEVER IS DEPRESSED, A DRAWER APPROACHES THE BIRD, BEARING ONE CIGARETTE IN A TROUGH. THE BIRD DIPS FORWARD, SYNCHRONIZING ITS MOVEMENT TO ARRIVE AT THE POINT WHERE THE CIGARETTE IS MOST EASILY SECURED. THE BIRD REVERTS TO AN UPRIGHT STANCE, CIGARETTE IN ITS BEAK, WHILE THE DRAWER RETRACTS. *THOMAS A. GRAY COLLECTION.*

81

BROWN AND WILLIAMSON

INTRODUCED THE

Willie the Penguin

countertop display

figure IN 1933. FOR 25

YEARS, HE SYMBOLIZED KOOL

CIGARETTES AND HAD

DOUBLED THEIR MARKET

82

SHARE BY THE TIME HE WAS

PHASED OUT IN 1958. THIS

MONOCLED, PAPIER-MACHÉ

VERSION WAS A COUNTERTOP

DISPLAY FIGURE THAT GRACED

MANY SMOKE SHOPS DURING

WILLIE'S LONG CAMPAIGN.

KAY TORNBORG COLLECTION.

A LONG GAIN
for throat comfort

HERE'S the smart play for smokers this season: block those hot cigarettes that scorch your throat. Signal for KOOLS! They're as far ahead on throat comfort as a forward pass is to a fumbled ball!

KOOLS are *mildly* mentholated. The mild menthol refreshingly cools the smoke, soothes your throat, while your tongue enjoys the hearty flavor of the fine Turkish-Domestic tobacco blend.

Cork-tipped; they don't stick to lips. Finally, each pack carries a B & W coupon good for worth-while nationally advertised premiums.

Throat just a wee bit dry and dusty? Here ...try a KOOL; refreshing as a rub-down between halves.

MILDLY MENTHOLATED

15¢

25¢ in Canada

CORK-TIPPED

KOOL
MILD MENTHOL
Cigarettes
CORK TIPPED

SAVE COUPONS FOR.... HANDSOME PREMIUMS

RALEIGH CIGARETTES...NOW DOWN TO POPULAR PRICES...ALSO CARRY B & W COUPONS

Swan ashtrays BY CHASE. AN ADVERTISEMENT ASSURES THAT THEY ARE
"SO DIFFERENT, THEY WILL STEAL THE CONVERSATION AT ANY BRIDGE TABLE."
POLISHED CHROME WITH EITHER RED OR BLACK HEAD.
PETER LINDEN & ERIC MENARD COLLECTION.

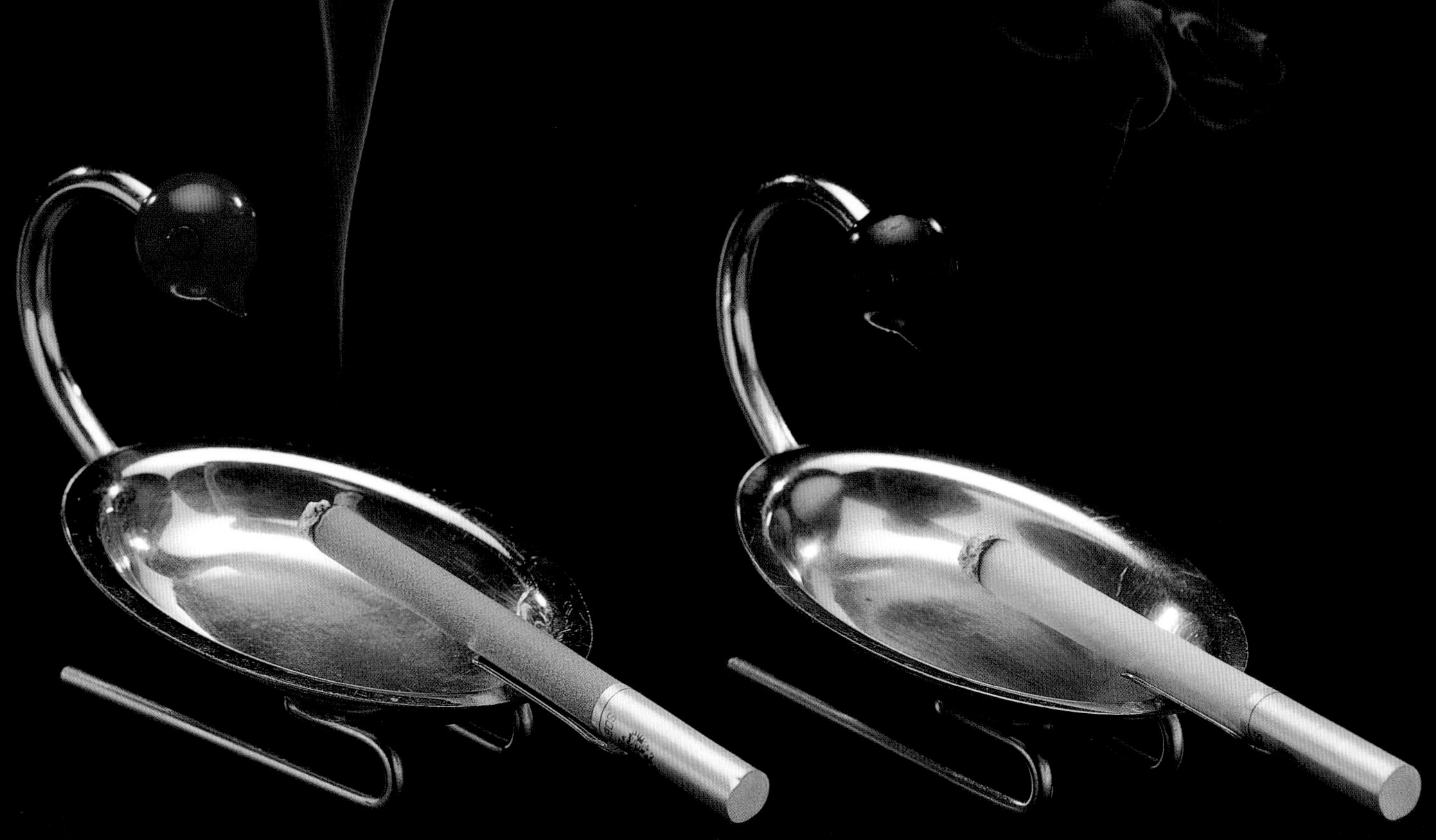

84

FOUR COLOR VARIATIONS OF THE "BANDBOX" MANUFACTURED BY CHASE

IN 1936. THESE **cigarette boxes** IN POLISHED CHROME AND COPPER OFFER

THREE WOOD-LINED COMPARTMENTS HOLDING TWENTY CIGARETTES EACH.

PETER LINDEN & ERIC MENARD COLLECTION.

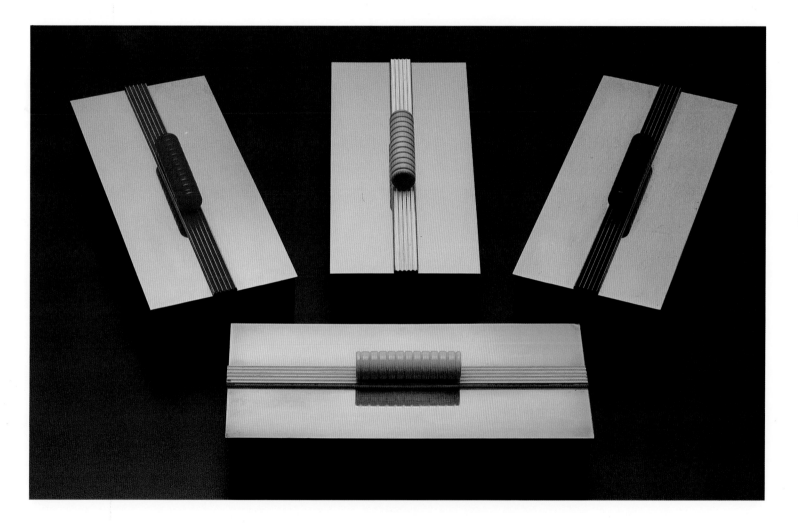

86

...and she gave
me a *ZIPPO*!

Love can't be totally blind . . . when it sees how clearly a ZIPPO lights the way to the masculine heart!

A man treasures his ZIPPO because it isn't just a fair-weather friend; a ZIPPO works in wind or wet with one quick zip. And he likes to know that ZIPPO offers free repair service for life.

When his ZIPPO's a gift from someone he loves, it's doubly dear to him.

ZIPPO
The World's
Best Loved
Lighter

Free lifetime service! No one has ever paid agent to have his Zippo repaired! **Leathercrafted, $6.00**

Zippo lighters work best with Zippo Lighter Fuel and sure-fire Zip-A-Flints. **Town & Country, $8.50**

Any Zippo with initials, signature or brief written message, only $1 extra. **Engine Turned, $5.75**

Ask your dealer to show you other handsome Zippo models, $3.50 and up. **14 Kt. Gold, $198.00**

Zippo lighter prices shown here include Federal Excise Tax. **Sports Series, $4.75**

©1953 ZIPPO MANUFACTURING COMPANY, Bradford, Pennsylvania • IN CANADA: ZIPPO MANUFACTURING CO. CANADA LTD., Niagara Falls, Ont. • *Prices slightly higher in Canada*

ORIGINATED IN 1932 BY GEORGE BLAISDELL, THE AMERICAN ZIPPO LIGHTER IS A QUINTESSENTIAL DESIGN. BASED UPON THE LINES OF AN AUSTRIAN ARMY LIGHTER, THE ZIPPO HAS FOSTERED MANY IMITATORS, BUT NO ONE HAS EQUALLED ITS STRENGTH AND DURABILITY. ¶ THESE EXAMPLES OF CURRENT DESIGN FEATURE A RARE "THREE SIDER" (SO NAMED FOR THE ILLUSTRATIONS APPEARING ON THREE OF THE FOUR LARGE SURFACES (LEFT); "ROUTE 66," MANUFACTURED BY ZIPPO EXCLUSIVELY FOR AN AUSTRALIAN NIGHT CLUB; AND A "DESERT SHIELD" COMMEMORATIVE EDITION (RIGHT). THE FLAT METAL SURFACES OF THE ZIPPO OFFER AN EASY OPPORTUNITY FOR CUSTOM ENGRAVING AND CORPORATE LOGOS. NO OTHER LIGHTER IN THE WORLD HAS SPORTED AS MANY LEGENDS AS ZIPPOS. *DICK STETTLER COLLECTION.*

An early Ronson family portrait.

Delight lighters from 1929: Jumbo (left),

Duplex (second left), Standard (center),

Princess (second right), and Junior (1928,

right). All offer monogram shields.

Dick Stettler Collection.

89

A POPULAR MOTIF FOR DESIGNERS OF
ART DECO PERIOD ACCESSORIES, **dice**
lighters ARE SEEN HERE IN LUCITE (LEFT),
UREA (CENTER), AND BAKELITE (RIGHT).
HARVEY SCHWARTZ COLLECTION.

A **six-sided sterling**

silver box FROM DUNHILL,

PARIS, C. 1935, SPORTS A

DOMINO MOTIF. PRESSURE

APPLIED TO THE "ONE"

RELEASES THE LID AND CAUSES

THE CIGARETTES TO RISE.

HARVEY SCHWARTZ COLLECTION.

THE **"Tower
Lighter,"** A PATENTED
DESIGN FROM CHASE, IS
COMPLIMENTED WITH AN
"ASH BALL," DESIGNED BY
WALTER VON NESSEN, THAT
SPORTS A CIGARETTE
"SNUFFER" ABOVE THE
CIGARETTE REST, ALSO
MANUFACTURED BY CHASE
IN 1940 (LEFT).
PETER LINDEN &
ERIC MENARD COLLECTION.

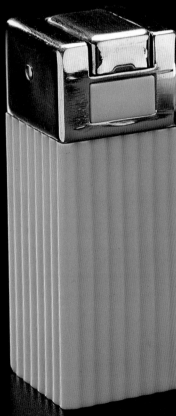

A COMMON SIGHT IN EUROPE, MATCH STRIKERS BORE SIMILAR ADVERTISING LEGENDS TO ASHTRAYS AND WERE A USUAL TABLETOP

ACCESSORY IN RESTAURANTS. THE SERRATIONS IN THE GLASS OR PORCELAIN WERE A CONVENIENT SCRATCHING SURFACE TO IGNITE A MATCH

THAT WAS STORED IN THE CENTRAL RECESS. THE GLASS HOLDERS, TRIMMED WITH STERLING SILVER, ARE OF UNKNOWN MANUFACTURE;

THE **porcelain striker and ashtray** IS JAPANESE MADE.

LEFT AND CENTER, DORIS LITTMAN COLLECTION. RIGHT, ROBERT AMRAM COLLECTION.

93

A 1928 **table lighter** MADE BY
DUNHILL FOR THE FRENCH MARKET
DWARFS TWO "OK" POCKET LIGHTERS
MANUFACTURED BY HILTON IN JAPAN, IN
THE MID-FIFTIES. THE EXAMPLE IN
OSTRICH SKIN IS WITHOUT FUEL (LEFT),
WHEREAS THE PIGSKIN MODEL IS FULL, AS
INDICATED BY THE WHITE "OK" LETTERS.
DICK STETTLER COLLECTION.

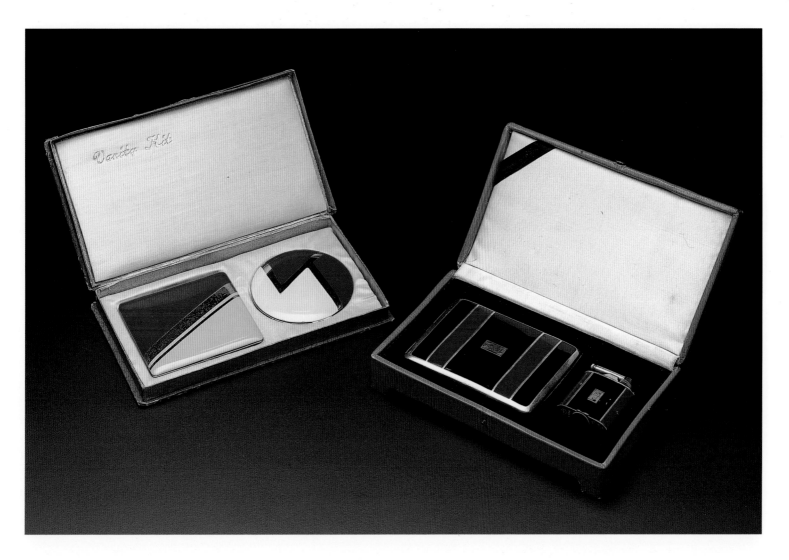

Smoking-related gift sets WERE POPULARIZED THROUGHOUT THE THIRTIES, FORTIES, AND FIFTIES BY COSMETICS COMPANIES AND LIGHTER AND CASE MANUFACTURERS, SOMETIMES COMBINING THEIR WARES TO PRODUCE "SETS": A HANDSOME GENTLEMAN'S SET BY MARATHON IN RED AND BLACK ENAMEL ON METAL (RIGHT); "VANITY KIT" FOR LADIES COMPOSED OF RED AND CREAM ENAMEL ON CHROME WITH A CIRCULAR COMPACT AND COMPLEMENTING CIGARETTE CASE, STRATTON, ENGLAND, C. 1934 (LEFT). *JUNE BERLINER COLLECTION.*

Table lighters,

EARLY FIFTIES, MANUFACTURED BY

THE AMERICAN SAFETY RAZOR COMPANY

IN BRASS PLATE AND COLORED

UREA PLASTIC.

A RARE **Ronson De-Light**

lighter lamp,

U.S. MANUFACTURE, 1929, IN

ENAMELLED METAL. FOR THE UP-

MARKET SMOKER.

DICK STETTLER COLLECTION.

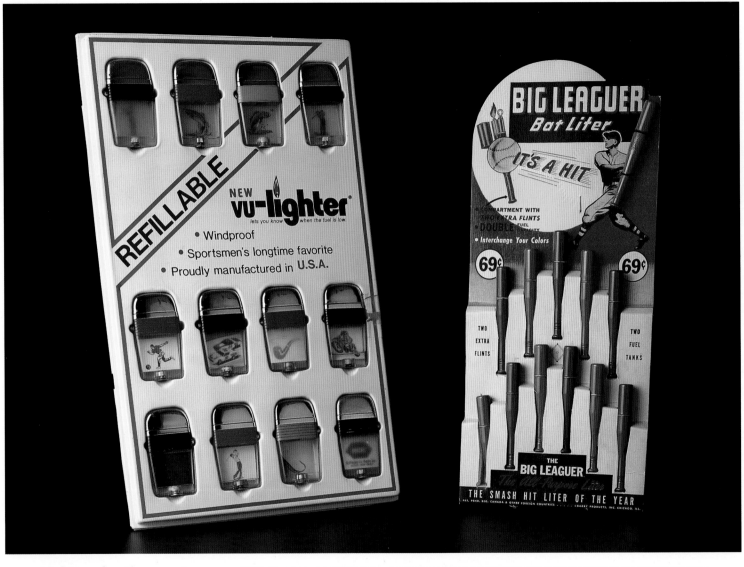

Lighters for the sportsman, C. 1959. THE SCRIPTO (USA) "VU-LIGHTER" AFFORDS SPORTSMEN THE OPPORTUNITY TO SEE WHEN THE FUEL

IS RUNNING LOW (LEFT). A CHROMIUM-PLATED BRASS CAP SURMOUNTS A CLEAR PLASTIC PETROL RESERVE WITH AN ILLUSTRATION OF THE SPORT OF CHOICE.

THE ALL-METAL BIG LEAGUER "BAT LITER" OFFERS TWO FUEL TANKS AND TWO SPARE FLINTS (RIGHT). *JUNE BERLINER COLLECTION.*

A **counter-top display** FEATURING THE FAMOUS **Ronson**

Touch tip table lighter (LEFT) WITH **pocket lighters**

FROM RONSON, C. 1948 (CENTER) AND 1938 (RIGHT). *LEFT, DISPLAY*

AND LIGHTER, COURTESY: PICCOLO PETE'S, SHERMAN OAKS.

CENTER, LIGHTER: AUTHOR COLLECTION.

RIGHT, LIGHTER: HARVEY SCHWARTZ COLLECTION.

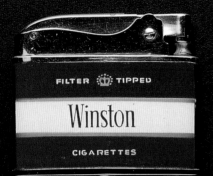
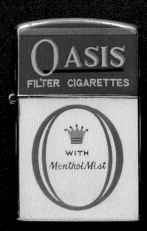

100

ENTHUSIASTICALLY EMBRACED

INEXPENSIVE **pocket lighters**

FROM JAPAN IN THE SIXTIES AND

SEVENTIES. THESE EXAMPLES ARE BY

CONTINENTAL (OASIS, PALL MALL,

CHESTERFIELD, AND L&M), CROWN

(WINSTON AND CAMEL), DELUXE

(TAREYTON), PENGUIN (SALEM), AND

RYAN (PHILIP MORRIS).

JUNE BERLINER COLLECTION.

101

102

"LOOSE-LEAF" TOBACCO WAREHOUSE IN TENNESSEE.

TOBACCO FIELD, MARIANNA, FLA.

ILLUSTRATIONS OF
A TOBACCO CROP
REPRODUCED AS
postcards
IN 1937.

CIGARETTE COMPANIES VIED FOR THE BIGGEST MARKET SHARE, EMPLOYING ANY MEDIUM THAT APPEARED USEFUL. **Postcards** DEPICTING COMPANY PLANTS WERE COMMONLY AVAILABLE IN NORTH CAROLINA.

AN **RCA "Microphone Radio"** IN THE SHAPE AND LOGO OF THE PARLIAMENT FILTER CIGARETTE PACK, C. 1955. MEASURING 13-1/2 INCHES HIGH, WITH A PLASTIC CABINET, THIS **AM** MODEL FEATURES A MICROPHONE, ENABLING YOUR VOICE TO BE AMPLIFIED THROUGH THE SET. A UNIQUE PROMOTIONAL ITEM. *AUTHOR COLLECTION.*

105

The **Porto Products' "Smokerette" Radio**, designed by the prestigious Chicago design house of Barnes & Reinecke, was available from 1947 onward. The Bakelite cabinet features recesses for four pipes, a large removable ashtray, two humidors for pipe tobacco and cigars, and two sections for cigarettes divided by an accommodation for matches.

The **Catalin plastic cigarette holder** (TOP LEFT) features the figure of Pirette, a popular Decorative Arts motif of the thirties.

RADIO: AUTHOR COLLECTION. CIGARETTE HOLDER: JUNE BERLINER COLLECTION. FORTIES PIPES, COURTESY: OFF THE WALL, LOS ANGELES.

A **glass and chrome cigarette server** OFFERING NEATLY STACKED CIGARETTES FOR TABLE OR DESKTOP USE. U.S., C. 1935.

109

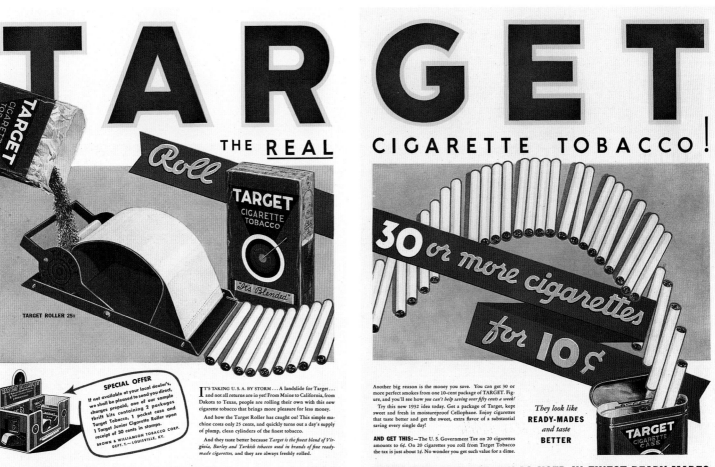

TARGET

THE <u>REAL</u> CIGARETTE TOBACCO!

Roll

TARGET
CIGARETTE
TOBACCO

"It's Blended"

TARGET ROLLER 25¢

30 or more cigarettes for 10¢

SPECIAL OFFER
If not available at your local dealer's, we shall be pleased to send you direct, charges prepaid, one of our sample thrift kits containing 2 packages Target Tobacco, 1 pocket case and 1 Target Junior Cigarette Roller upon receipt of 30 cents in stamps.
BROWN & WILLIAMSON TOBACCO CORP.
DEPT. T.— LOUISVILLE, KY.

IT'S TAKING U. S. A. BY STORM . . . A landslide for Target . . . and not all returns are in yet! From Maine to California, from Dakota to Texas, people are rolling their own with this new cigarette tobacco that brings more pleasure for less money.

And how the Target Roller has caught on! This simple machine costs only 25 cents, and quickly turns out a day's supply of plump, clean cylinders of the finest tobacco.

And they taste better because *Target is the finest blend of Virginia, Burley and Turkish tobacco used in brands of fine ready-made cigarettes,* and they are always freshly rolled.

Another big reason is the money you save. You can get 30 or more perfect smokes from one 10-cent package of TARGET. Figure, and you'll see how *you can't help saving over fifty cents a week!*

Try this new 1932 idea today. Get a package of Target, kept sweet and fresh in moistureproof Cellophane. Enjoy cigarettes that taste better and get the sweet, extra flavor of a substantial saving every single day!

AND GET THIS:—The U. S. Government Tax on 20 cigarettes amounts to 6¢. On 20 cigarettes you roll from Target Tobacco the tax is just about 1¢. No wonder you get such value for a dime.

They look like
READY-MADES
and taste
BETTER

TARGET
CIGARETTE
CASE

40 GUMMED CIGARETTE PAPERS FREE WITH EACH PACKAGE

SAME KIND AND QUALITY AS USED IN FINEST READY-MADES

THIS U.S.-MADE **temple-form dispenser** IS CHROMED METAL WITH LUCITE COLUMNS AND A GLASS WINDOW.

IT OFFERS SINGLE CIGARETTES AT THE PUSH OF A SMALL LEVER AT THE RIGHT HAND SIDE, C. 1925.

THOMAS A. GRAY COLLECTION.

112

A lady's combined cigarette case and

compact WITH LIGHTER, LIPSTICK BRUSH, AND,
INCREDIBLY, A SMALL FLASHLIGHT SECRETED AT THE END
OF ONE TUBE. THE PLASTIC IS A LIGHT SWIRLED UREA.
A MID-FIFTIES SET FROM REVELL PLASTICS, HOLLYWOOD,
CALIFORNIA. *JUNE BERLINER COLLECTION.*

114

A **rectangular desk box** DESIGNED BY MANNING BOWMAN IN THE EARLY THIRTIES PLAYS HOST TO AN ASSORTMENT OF DOLL'S HOUSE SMOKING

FURNISHINGS AND ACCESSORIES IN VARIOUS MINIATURE SCALES, THE SMALLEST (RONSON TABLE LIGHTER FACSIMILE, BOTTOM RIGHT) MEASURING 1/8 INCH IN

LENGTH. DETAIL: A) **Ashstand.** B) **Ashtray.** C) **Tobacco jar.** D) **Match holder.** E) **Ashtray.** F) **Lucky Strike cigarette pack.**

G) **Tobacco jar.** H) **Matchbox.** I) **Ashtray.** J) **matchbox.** K) **Ronson table lighter.**

BOX: *JUNE BERLINER COLLECTION. ACCESSORIES: KAY TORNBORG COLLECTION.*

The "Rollaround" cigarette box OFFERED SPACE FOR 80 CIGARETTES, AND WAS NAMED FOR ITS ABILITY TO BE ROLLED ACROSS A FLAT TABLE SURFACE ON ITS CORNER BALL BEARING MOUNTS. FINISHED IN SATIN NICKEL, IT HAS A LID ETCHED IN CONCENTRIC CIRCLES WITH A TWO-TONE CATALIN PLASTIC HANDLE. MANUFACTURED BY CHASE IN 1933.
PETER LINDEN & ERIC MENARD COLLECTION.

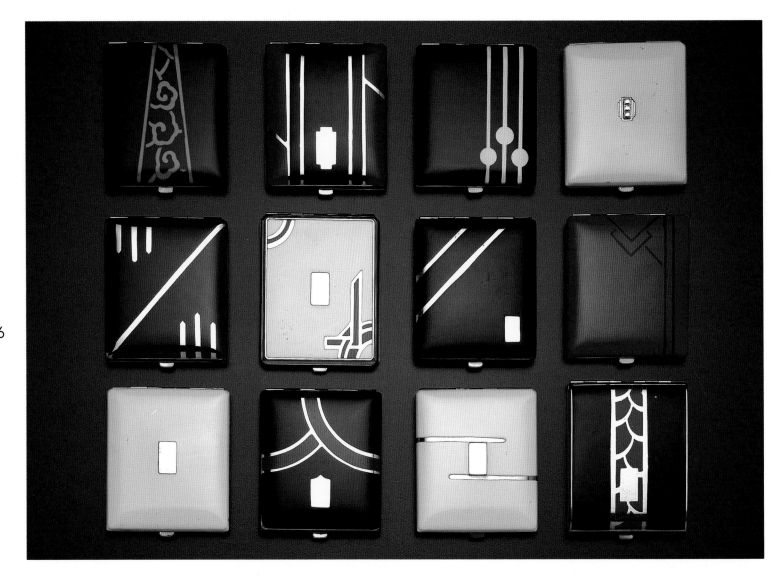

WOMEN SMOKERS WERE OFFERED A WIDE VARIETY OF **cigarette cases**. BLACKER BROTHERS AND THE MARATHON COMPANY PROVIDED A GREAT NUMBER. PRODUCED IN THE U.S. THROUGH THE THIRTIES AND FORTIES, THEY BECAME A NORMAL ACCESSORY IN ANY PURSE. THESE CASES, ENAMELLED ON METAL IN A VARIETY OF COLORS, WERE INEXPENSIVE GIFT ITEMS. MANY BEAR A MONOGRAM SHIELD. *JUNE BERLINER COLLECTION.*

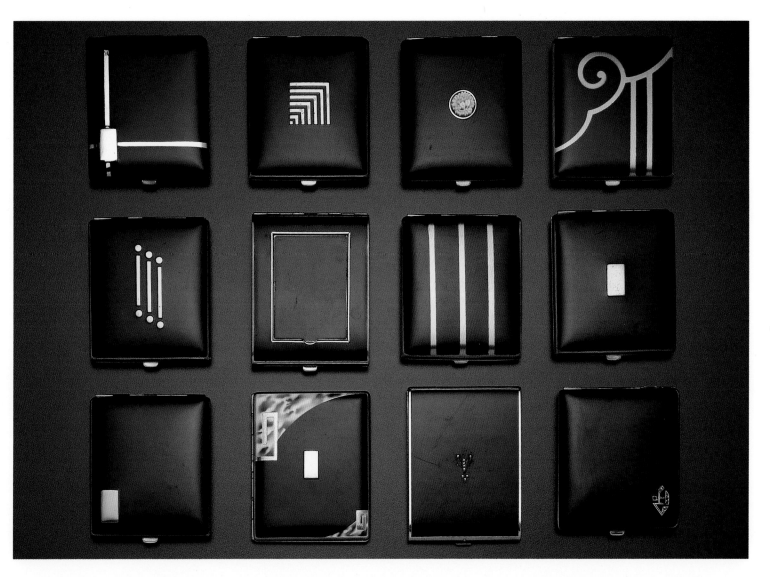

A SELECTION OF **cigarette cases** WITH ART DECO DESIGNS FROM THE THIRTIES IN BLACK FEATURING VARIOUS CHROME AND GILT EMBELLISHMENTS, MANUFACTURED IN THE U.S. BY BLACKER BROTHERS, RHODE ISLAND, AND THE MARATHON COMPANY. BLACK WAS THE PREFERRED COLOR FOR EVENING AND FORMAL SOCIAL FUNCTIONS, AND THE LITTLE BLACK CASE RANKED WITH THE LITTLE BLACK DRESS FOR THE FASHIONABLE FLAPPER. *JUNE DERLINER COLLECTION.*

A

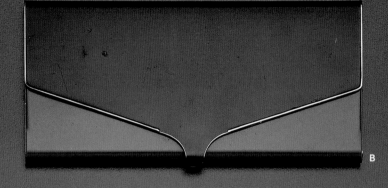

B

C

D

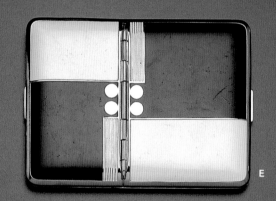

E

F

G

H

I

118

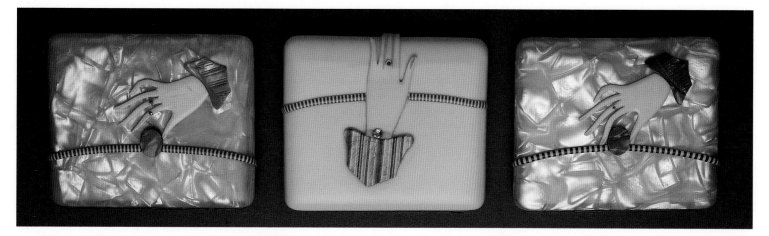

French ladies' cigarette cases IN PEARLESCENT CELLULOID (LEFT AND RIGHT) AND SOLID CREAM CELLULOID (CENTER). THE HAND MOTIF GRIPPING THE CASE PERIMETER (CENTER) IS FUNCTIONAL, THE FINGERS SERVING AS A CLASP TO SECURE CLOSURE, C. 1930. *JUNE BERLINER COLLECTION.*

Ladies' cigarette cases FROM 1896 TO THE LATE THIRTIES. TWO GERMAN EXAMPLES FEATURE A PEASANT BOY SMOKING, FINISHED IN BAKED ENAMEL ON METAL, C. 1935 (A), AND ENAMELLED PORTRAIT ON STERLING SILVER, C. 1900 (C). TWO SLIM CASES FROM THE LATE THIRTIES TAKE THE FORM OF A SYMMETRICAL PURSE, ENAMELLED ON METAL, MADE BY BLACKER, USA (B AND H). TWO SMALL CASES BY MARATHON, USA, AGAIN ENAMELLED ON METAL, OFFER A MONOGRAM SHIELD, CENTER, MANUFACTURED IN THE EARLY THIRTIES (D AND F). A COMBINATION CIGARETTE CASE AND COMPACT WAS MANUFACTURED BY RICHARD HUDNUT, USA, IN FAMILIAR ART DECO BLACK AND WHITE PATTERN ENAMELLED ON METAL (E), AND AN ENGLISH BRASS CASE FEATURES A GRAPHIC ON FOIL OF FROLICKING LADIES, FINELY DETAILED, UNDER A CLEAR CELLULOID LENS (G). A JOYFUL HORSERACING SCENE ADORNS AN 1896 CASE FROM ENGLAND, "KING EDWARD AT THE RACES" (PROBABLY ASCOT) (I). ENAMELLED ON STERLING SILVER, THE SCENE CELEBRATES THE KING'S HORSE BEING LED INTO THE WINNER'S ENCLOSURE. FINE DETAIL REVEALS A GOLD TASSLE TOPPING OFF THE JOCKEY'S HAT—THE SOLE DEPARTURE FROM CORRECT SILKS AND A COURTESY EXTENDED BY THE JOCKEY CLUB TO A REIGNING ENGLISH MONARCH. *JUNE BERLINER COLLECTION.*

120

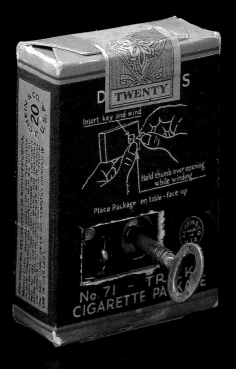
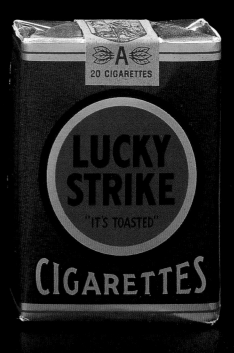

"I protect my voice with LUCKIES"

"It's that delightful taste after a cup of coffee that makes Luckies a hit with me. And naturally I protect my voice with Luckies. No harsh irritants for me...I reach for a Lucky instead. **Congratulations on your improved Cellophane wrapper. I can open it.**"

Edmund Lowe

Who can forget **Edmund Lowe** as "**Sergeant Quirt**" in "**What Price Glory?**" That mighty role made Eddie famous in filmland—and he's more than held his own in a long line of talkie triumphs. We hope you saw him in the "**Spider.**" And be sure to see him in the **Fox** thriller, "**The Cisco Kid.**"

MOISTURE-
PROOF
CELLOPHANE
*Sealed Tight
Ever Right*
THE UNIQUE
HUMIDOR
PACKAGE
Zip—
and it's open!

LUCKY STRIKE
it's toasted
CIGARETTES

"It's toasted"

Your Throat Protection — against irritation — against cough

And Moisture-Proof Cellophane Keeps that "Toasted" Flavor Ever Fresh

Copr., 1931,
The American
Tobacco Co.

★ **Is Mr. Lowe's State-ment Paid For?**

You may be interested in knowing that not one cent was paid to Mr. Lowe to make the above statement. Mr. Lowe has been a smoker of LUCKY STRIKE cigarettes for 6 years. We hope the publicity herewith given will be as beneficial to him and to Fox, his producers, as his endorsement of LUCKIES is to you and to us.